VIEWS FROM MOUNT ATHOS

Searching for forgotten
Christian knowledge of man
among the monks of Mount Athos,
the Holy Mountain of Northern Greece.

by Robin Amis

"Jesus said: 'Let him who seeks not cease seeking until he finds, and when he finds, he will be troubled, and when he has been troubled he will marvel, and he will reign over the All.'" (Gospel According to Thomas)

PRAXIS

Published by

PRAXIS INSTITUTE PRESS

Chicago, USA, and Bristol, England
© 2014 Praxis Research Institute Inc.
All rights reserved

For information, contact Praxis Research Institute,
9A Royal York Crescent, Courtyard Flat, Bristol, BS8 4JZ, England
Email: info@praxisresearch.net
Website: www.praxisresearch.net

British Library Cataloging in Publication Data:
Amis, Robin
Views From Mount Athos
I. Title   II. Amis, Robin
ISBN 978-1-872292-32-8

Photo Credits: (RA) Robin Amis, (MG) Monastery Gregoriou

DEDICATION

Spiritual men seek among the centuries-old forests of Athos - the Holy Mountain of Northern Greece - for ten or a dozen holy men who are sanctified to replace a similar number in the hidden corners of Athos' forests and mountains. When these secret-saints die, it is said, ten or twelve new saints are formed, although at any time, only two of them become publicly known. I was blessed to meet one of them on a number of occasions, sometimes being able to find a translator of his Greek, sometimes being forced to learn through the language of love without detailed interpretation. Both ways, it seemed to me that I learned then 'by heart', not just in words, but in new understanding.

– Robin Amis

CONTENTS

PREFACE

The world-war was over. Whole areas of London lay in ruins, and the city was still almost war-dark at night, and almost empty of people, the returned combatants still wanting only to stay home with their families. A few people came and went. In parts of the empty city-center that were almost unmarked by war, some thirty or more young men and women gathered in the evenings and began questioning. They had missed going to university because they were not properly prepared, their families were bankrupted by two wars, and the soldiers had first-call on university places.

They began not by questioning a ruined society, but by questioning-themselves, not by drinking alcohol, but in the coffee-bars that were beginning to spring up in the city: the Nucleus, Bunjies, and small, cheap restaurants. They formed plans for their seedling-lives, for which no seed-bed had been prepared. Each tested this and that occupation, until in time they discovered something they could do that was useful, and which earned a couple-of-pounds a week which would pay tube-fares and buy a cheap meal. They were, by accident, non-specialists in a world forced into specialization by two wars in less than half-a-century. They asked the questions of non-specialists, but without tutors, discussion-groups organized by their elders, or any of the elaborate education facilities that non-specialists of the previous or later decades received.

As one of these non-specialists, turning to discover ourselves and also, in my case, to discover the roots of our failed-civilization, my own solution was to turn my investigation towards the earliest form of Christianity I could find.

In this, the least-changed remnant of the original faith that was accessible to me I discovered on Mount Athos, the still-feudal monastic community on a mountainous peninsula of Northern Greece, and it was there that I found not only friends with common understanding, but also, answers to my questions. This book describes some of those answers. For example, the doorbell that once rang when I first visited the *Skete* of Saint Andrew and obtained no answer was symptomatic of the long-silent church-bells of Saint Andrews. It represents the appeal our hearts make to our own selves, an appeal most people in the modern world have forgotten how to answer, for today we forget that we habitually protect our hearts from displeasure, and because we forget this, we wonder why we feel no joy!

We have forgotten our hearts by selling ourselves for the security of a steady income: sacrificed our talents for the comforts that technology can bring, fixed our future in trustee-investments that bind our lives instead of setting us free – and in all these ways we wonder why nothing new happens to us!

This book presents an alternative.

INTRODUCTION

Sunset on Mount Athos (RA)

Exploring the Holy Mountain is exploring oneself

This book will present the reader with a few challenges – firstly because it is difficult to place it into a category. Is it a travel diary? Is it a pilgrim's personal philosophy? Is it a description of a strange and foreign place and its inhabitants? And even more difficult: does it follow a logical time-sequence?

All these are valid questions – but they don't help us very much to define exactly what this book is. Like all accounts of the more intense experiences in one's life – the time element gets blurred – one event overlaps another, sometimes in sequence – sometimes not. In this text, you can be reading about the author's second visit, and suddenly you are jumped ahead to the seventh – then a few chapters on, dragged right back to the first!

The keenly observed descriptions of landscape and monasteries are interspersed with deeply learned 'lessons' – truths brought home to the author by circumstances which so often evoked an inner response.

It is these revelations which tie the book together – and as in all true revelations, they do not follow a logical sequential pattern – they come 'out of the blue,' surfacing when another relevant memory calls them up into consciousness out of the depths of our being. The book, then, could really be called an 'inner journey,' for which external details provide a kind of scaffolding on which to hang the various insights that keep on emerging all the way from the beginning of the book to its end.

Much of what is written in this book derives from remembered conversations with monks on the Mountain. As a result, many of the quotes are without exact references, since many are drawn from an ancient 'oral tradition.' This is one of the elements which differentiates this very personal account from an academic treatise.

The history of this book itself seems a trifle mysterious. It was originally written in 1988, after the author had completed about a dozen of his lengthy visits to the Holy Mountain – visits which first began in 1982.

What started as a sort of travel diary became fleshed-out into a true remembrance of each visit – giving the writing the quality and freshness of first impressions – the immediacy of innocent eyes viewing a totally foreign and exotic land whose inhabitants were even more strange and unknown.

This quality of just how strange his first encounters with the Holy Mountain must have seemed to him is encapsulated in an introduction by the late Donald Hamilton Fraser, RA, to a small book of poetry written by Robin Amis in the '60's. *"Even my first meeting with Amis was more metaphor than social encounter. I was spending a night as a guest at the Greek Orthodox monastery of Simonos Petra on Mount Athos. As I was being welcomed by the monks I saw, through a doorway that led on to a high balcony, the unlikely figure of a man dressed as if for an evening walk in the Gloucestershire countryside. He was gazing through the haze of the setting sun towards the great triangular profile of Mount Athos itself. Although an Englishman out of context, I sensed an odd inevitability about his presence there. I was intrigued to know what had brought him to such a place and why he seemed to be strangely at ease there, so at home on the Holy Mountain. Now that I have read his poems the answer is clearer than it has ever been...*

"His poems are full of questions. Of course, it is in the nature of young poets to ask questions but, whereas most leave those questions hanging gracefully in the air, Amis chose to set his poetry aside and to embark on the hard road of seeking real answers. Such an undertaking involves 'courage locked into a profound integrity of purpose' as a commentator on the French poet Rene Daumal once put it. 'The poetic sensibility must be borne into the drier climate of the intellect. A desert crossed, the dryness endured, disappointments faced, yet questions intact.'

"Yet, a certain moment may come to those who have lasted the journey when a door opens and the almost forgotten questions find their answers. Perhaps this is the 'door to summer firm beneath winter snow' that Amis speaks of in one of his best poems. The door that connects the chamber of the mind with the chamber of the heart, the door leading to wholeness and reconciliation." (Who Writes the Waves, Agora/Praxis Press, 1992)

This relation of mind to heart forms the basis of this book, as well as much of Amis' writing over the years.

He himself once described his first visit to the Holy Mountain of Athos in this way: *"When I was younger, I had the subjective experience of finding myself in an immense and beautiful cathedral. I was awestruck by its scale and beauty – and would have been overjoyed but for one thing – the fact that I found myself totally alone in this space – and what a sense of loneliness it was!*

"Then, years later, when I first visited Mount Athos, I again found myself in this same holy-place – except for one difference – this time, it was inhabited!"

This book was actually written in 1988, and then, in a series of moves, both in England and abroad, for the next twenty years, the draft of the manuscript was set-aside because at that time it did not seem suitable for its readership. One effect of having to move house constantly was that the manuscript disappeared and was forgotten.

Then, a few months ago (in June 2013), when the author was just completing the last pages of another and far more difficult book and which had already taken four years to write, this manuscript was suddenly rediscovered in the archives. It emerged – as the finder said – with all the newness and vitality of a green-shoot sprouting out of the earth. The fact that it was almost complete, ready to print and go out into the world in just a matter of weeks, makes it even more miraculous.

Because this book was originally written in 1988, it naturally reflects the Greece of that time – a Greece which, in those twenty-five years, has changed almost beyond recognition. But the heartwarming thing, and the confirmation of all he writes, is that in this time, the Holy Mountain itself has very-little changed, the friends he made there then are still his friends today, and the truths its community embodies retain their quality of eternal-truth.

– LGA, 2013

View of Gregoriou Monastery from the seashore (RA)

CHAPTER I

THE SEARCH BEGINS

My investigation into Athos, my pilgrimages to the Holy Mountain, really began when I received in the post a typescript copy of a talk between a visiting Englishman and a monk on the Holy Mountain of Athos. The whole extraordinary conversation – in which the visitor had been given information which clearly shaped the direction of his life, began by describing an earlier conversation on Mount Athos. At that time, I had never been further east than Paris, yet the strange thing was that I felt as if I recognized the speaker by the way that he spoke.

It was like remembering a long-forgotten friend ... with all the happiness this can involve. I could never justify this statement intellectually. I did not then know this monk, or his monastery, or even the person to whom he had been speaking. Who could it be that his words reminded me of? My mind turned back to the time several years before, when I had begun to read about Mount Athos.

I read that the monk of Athos was once told by an inner voice to *"keep thy soul in hell, and despair not,"* … and the effort to do so had clearly been a major factor in the change that made a simple peasant into a saint. In this phrase lives the whole essence of monasticism. Now, in finding signs of another such man, I was becoming aware of something which was to change the direction of my own life. Such men have a special significance in the religion of Mount Athos, for the key to Athonite religion is not in concept and doctrine, but in the way a person's being determines their actions. On Athos there are certain men known as elders: men who have persisted long in certain spiritual practices. Their very nature has been transformed as a result.

Such men rarely exist in everyday Western society. Even in our many churches, such men are incredibly rare if they exist at all. On Athos such a man is regarded as an *'elder.'* The word is, in Russian, *'starets,'* in Greek, *'geron,'* a term often used for the Abbot of an Athos monastery, such as Father George of the 700 year old monastery of Gregoriou: an old man, a man of deep experience.

Clearly, there is more to being a *geron* than mere age ... the difference can be fully understood only by experience – only by meeting such a man.

But the paradox of Athos is that here, repeatedly, the possibility of a change for the better is found in things that are unchanging, and in the recognition that the same change of 'personality' had been revealed in the words of two different men. Here I was, without at first realizing it, touching on two of the great mysteries of Christianity. One is the mystery of redemption, the other the innermost meaning of *paradocis:* the Orthodox Christian concept of tradition.

FIRST VISIT – DEPARTURE

Weighed down by papers, and with ankles thickened and blotched red by mosquitoes, we left the ancient Greek city of Thessaloníki early in the day, heading for Ouranoupolis *('Heaven City,'* population seven hundred, with 2,000 plus beds 'in season'), a four-hour, hundred-and-forty-kilometre bus journey, first across the dry Macedonian-plain, then winding high into the oak-and-chestnut-forested Holomondas mountains, back down onto the more hospitable coastal plain, and on, to the lowland connecting to the Akti Peninsula on which Mount Athos is situated. In Ouranoupolis, we gathered more information, together with some of the many items that experienced Athos travelers suggested. Map. Matches to light the oil-lamps. Medical-supplies. A small reserve of food.

Finally, Sunday, September the nineteenth 1982, was the day. I had once again passed through the initial problems, overcoming my unwillingness to travel to unfamiliar places, and to trust myself to an unfamiliar and in some ways archaic culture. Overcome once, resistances may become weaker, but they must be overcome many times before they disappear. Yet these unwillingnesses are the pilgrim's greatest strength. How could one grow if one had nothing to give up?

At this stage, I had only made initial efforts to open up communication with the monks upon the mountain. I regarded these as the first two steps or stages on my 'pilgrim's way.'

One thing I quickly discovered on this way is that, allied to our overall Western habit of wanting always to predict and control our environment, modern man is a slave to comfort. Yet if you give up your comfort once on the path of pilgrimage, you find you must give it up a thousand times.

Before all this, I once played a part in a research programme which showed a clear 'correlation' in individuals between a dogmatic need for certainty and what, in our Western world, are called 'neurotic states.' Now this was confirmed for me in a more personal way, as I discovered how a constant repetition of the need to give up our certainties can, like dripping water, wear its own path through the stone of our worldly hearts. By this repetition, one briefly enters the path of the monk in an inward way, even when we must remain committed to the world outwardly.

It is change of heart, *metanoia*, nowadays translated repentance, which is most important. One may fall short of the monk's self-conquest externally, and it does not matter. What matters is cleaning the 'inside of the cup.'

"Thou blind Pharisee, cleanse first that which is within the cup and platter, that the outside of them may be clean also." (Matthew 23:26)

With God's help, we have to do what we cannot do unaided: to challenge and eventually to break the power of what the Fathers called *peirasmos,* in its sense of *'temptation from the devil;'* to overcome in ourselves our habits, delusions, and desires. *"Lead us not into temptation, but deliver us from evil."* (Matthew 6:13) As we are tested by external trials – the personal problems that probe and reveal our weaknesses – these habits are revealed to us, and it is then, and not until then, that, by God's grace, we may begin to free ourselves from them.

Thus even a firm decision to go on pilgrimage, to take a journey as a pilgrimage and not as holiday, has its own special effect. It is a limited time death-to-the-world: a commitment that for a period of time acts as the equivalent of the monk's monastic profession. Only this, I believe, may qualify one to enter the special world of the monk and then talk to him in the language of experience: a tongue that remains unknown to the uncommitted.

And this also has one other particular effect, an effect I am sure known also to most of the monks on the Holy Mountain: it is this which turns the challenges of life, of travel, into something more, something by which one comes to know oneself better. In a sense, it divides us into two people. One is a 20th century man grappling with the difficulties, while the other, the monk inside, looks on, learns, begins to taste that *lypis,* that sorrow for one's sins that is the secret of Athos' ability to maintain a single truth over more than a thousand years of changing faces.

So, slowly, too slowly, the monk inside us begins to become one with the previously forgetful man of the world, to become a cause of remembering again what is too easily forgotten. For forgetting: the forgetting of purpose, of objectives, of standards, is the main characteristic of our modern life.

FIRST IMPRESSIONS

Agiou Pantaleimonos (Witold Rawicz (PL))

First impressions were of the enormous size of the main monasteries, especially Panteleimon, the Russian monastery on the Southwest shore of the peninsula, which supposedly held two or three thousand monks in its heyday (reports of the exact number vary considerably). A year or two back, it held about thirty; now the number is even less. At Panteleimon, one can clearly see that many of the barrack-like buildings are partly in ruins. Although the 'Kremlin-domes' of the main churches shine with recent gold, many of the massive buildings are not so lucky. Some have no roofs.

Balconies sag, doors bang in the wind, weeds creep between the blocks that once housed chanting monks, and a hundred stone-mullioned windows in regimented rows gaped glassless to the Grecian sky, as the ferry fussed along to the *arsanas* of Xeropotamou, the monastery just before the little port of Dafni, where all the mail for Athos was put ashore: seven large bags. The volume of mail was noticeably large for the mountain, compared with what seemed then a very small volume of goods being shipped in and out. But surely, this is a significant sign that what now, since the invasion of Tibet, must be the world's only 'land dedicated to the Spirit,' is not entirely without outside communication.

REMEMBERING

Remembering is funny: to remember what we might be, instead of acting as we habitually act, we must sacrifice our habits: must take up the cross, accept our imperfections. Here, in modern guise, is *'Agni,'* the ancient sacrificial fire of the Hindu Upanishads; *'aesch mezareph,'* the *'purifying fire'* or secret fire of the alchemists.

It must be fed continually, and into it, piece by piece, must go our past. Only thus do we remember ourselves in the present.

On this journey, as I have already outlined, the problems – and the opportunities – which began for me at Thessaloníki, generated a constant friction, a continual necessity to give up, especially to give up all illusion about oneself, to go beyond the comfortable limits of life as I had grown to expect it. By the time I stepped for the first time onto the boat to Athos, the unfamiliar was already beginning to become a way of life.

For one as untraveled as myself, this constant friction helped, firstly, to make it possible for me to go through with my journey, and then, secondly, it caused the events of the journey to acquire a symbolic significance out of all proportion to their meaningfulness to someone accustomed to local conditions, local transport, and the local attitudes to time. Finally, as can only become clear later in this book, it led me to understand that it is not instruction; it is friction which gives rise to self-knowledge.

On the boat to Athos, the uncertainty already aroused by the unfamiliarities of Greece was greatly intensified from the moment when I found myself aboard the crowded ferry.

The decks and the rickety seating of this otherwise modern eighty-foot boat carried upwards of a hundred monks, priests, and laymen, the monks sitting in inward-turned groups and chattering vociferously. The tourists and 'new' pilgrims, looking toward the shore, were mostly silent, the real newcomers visibly-apprehensive: fidgeting, smoking too heavily, talking too loud.

When the alarm-clock had sounded, a little before 6 am that day, we were already awake, and the first sounds of small fishing boats were coming through the shutters in the pre-dawn greyness. The ferry was due to depart at seven, so I dressed and finished packing my small shoulder-bag quickly.

After a quick breakfast at the pavement taverna by the quay, I joined the throng of monks, pilgrims, and tourists waiting for the boat to load. A gray-uniformed policeman collected passports and passes, leaving me feeling even more vulnerable as I surrendered to him my legal existence in this unfamiliar world.

It was about ten-past-seven when the white steel boat actually pulled out, heading down the coast towards the distant tip of the Athos peninsula.

On the journey to Dafni, the 'port' of Athos, about two-thirds of the way along the peninsula, the boat traveled close to the rocky beaches and often precipitous sides of Athos, taking about one and a half hours, with brief 'touch and go' stops at the 'arsenals' or fortified jetties of several monasteries to put monks ashore, and to transfer their often large and untidy plastic or string-and-cardboard packages.

CHANGE OF HEART

As the purpose of this book is to talk not only about the scenery of the Holy Mountain, which is so aptly described elsewhere, but about ideas and their application in practice, so, at this stage in the book, I shall try to explain the ideas I introduce. For instance, the possibility, the proof of redemption, lies hid in the evidence that under some conditions, men can change in fundamental ways. These special kinds of change can be encapsulated in the idea of change-of-heart.

The evidence for this is enshrined in the icons of the saints, in the words of the *geron,* in the shining eyes of the hermit who lives deprived of normal human comfort, and all these things are found on Athos.

On Athos, too, I discovered, lies a more direct contact with the tradition of the Early Fathers who shaped the First Church to come into being in Europe. The roots of this tradition themselves lie – as I was to discover – in this possibility that one can change one's heart, as well as one's mind, a possibility which I first began to see manifested on Athos. These facts have echoed down the centuries, and continue to over-run the hardened boundaries of the individual personality. So we can say that it is easy to change the mind, but then it can change back again. Changing the heart is more difficult, but for this reason, it is more constant. It is this difficult-to-achieve change of heart that is often lacking in modern methods of 'self-realization,' because this is not something that we can invent for ourselves, as it is not normally within our control.

PHILOXENIA

Here on Athos, the Byzantine idea lingers-on in strange contrasts. Along with the most ascetic cooking, you meet *'philoxenia,'* the rich hospitality that shapes and expresses the Greek character, and which is so aptly expressed in the icon of the Trinity. Of course, one also finds what sometimes seems to be genuine Byzantine plumbing: in the monasteries best-placed to utilize the torrents from the mountains, anachronistic DIY plastic-piping puts constant running-water to work in the darkest recesses of massive old buildings.

But Athos is not just these great monasteries, little-changed after seven-hundred years, so that they still look like walled medieval towns, and some of their architecture looks like the illustrations of Roman cities they had in textbooks when I was at school. Athos is also steeply wooded hillsides, ageless vineyards and olive-groves, bleak shoulders of storm-scoured rock, veins of white-marble, hermits caves with skulls tucked away in niches, or which are walled-off with ancient stone, its joints hardly visible, to become the hidden tomb of some anchorite left in the place where he came close to God. Athos is enormous monasteries seen beside small, isolated *kellia* and *sketes:* communities of a few monks, friends whose sole aim is to be alone with God.

Then there is Karyes, a town populated only by men: half ghost town with its many empty-looking buildings, half administrative-center, its police-station, its Holy-Community building, its hotels – about which I shall say more later – and the few untidy shops which form the main source of supply for the monks.

Here, in Karyes, even the tailor and the shoemaker are monks. The gift-shop was attended by a monk in his seventies with a flowing white beard who, when I once asked him the way to one of the houses in the town, walked a hundred yards from his still open shop before I could get him to accept that now I could manage on my own. It is here, above all, amongst these strange contrasts, that the ideas, and even the practices of those Desert Fathers who did so much to shape and preserve the Christianity of Byzantium live on today. Such ideas are still at home in these beautiful but rugged forests and cliffs, many of which look out from Northern Greece, across the 'Holy Sea' to Turkey, modern occupier of the heartland of ancient Byzantium herself.

HERMITAGES AND SKETES

The Desert Fathers would have been at home here, especially in Karoulia, the 'desert' slope that runs steeply to the sea at the tip of Athos. This is as difficult of access, and as little supplied with water, shade, or fertile-soil, as any desert Sketis of old.

In those hermitages, and in the monasteries which keep constant relation with them, is a world I had believed long-dead, a world where men care more for God than for their own comfort, and where an Abbot, even today, can forbid – on his still considerable domains – any four-wheeled machine, lest the monastery becomes approachable by traffic, and the spirit be subordinated to the letter in this ancient principality of a slower way of life, one that is now long-dead throughout the rest of Europe.

Not only are the words of these holy monks and hermits still preserved here, but here they are translated into modern Greek, and here their translators into other tongues find support and guidance even today. Yet greater than the preservation of their words, is the proper practical expression of that rich-river of experience that has en-souled Christianity, at least since the third-century AD, and which has flourished on the fertile slopes of Athos for at least a thousand years.

A DIFFERENT SCIENCE

In a remarkably short time, exposure to this different world had turned my Western view of life on its head. By its very nature, the scientific idea of the 'repeatable experiment' tests only things we can control. Our science is therefore underlain and motivated by the desire for control. It visualizes the world in terms of our aim to control everything.

Because of this, we now lack any clear way to understand or trust experience which does not occur under our control.

As a result, our science, I discovered, is just one kind of science, an active science, which solved every problem by 'doing' something about it.

The result is what Galbraith called *'the age of uncertainty,'* a civilization which, based on our fear of the unknown, engenders a cruel ethos of competition and conflict. Reflecting this situation, our society finds it impossible to understand the monks of Athos, the best of whom, like all true men of faith, do not allow themselves to be driven by this fear.

Such men today still change beyond-belief, and do so for no purely-external cause. Yet it would not be correct to say that the Holy Mountain is 'unscientific.'

It would be truer to say that Athos expresses its own kind of knowledge, its own spiritual-science, and does so by forcing us to relinquish control: by making us leave the important things to God. This inner-science of Mount Athos is based on its own kind of evidence, which conforms to different-rules so that it takes the form of inner-experience; of revelations-recognized. One of the principles of this science is that such evidence is often unpredictable. Also, it is often available only to people one-at-a-time.

However, certain predictions are possible. St. Hesychios, one of the Early Fathers of the Church, and a true 'scientist of the Spirit,' said:

> *"Just as controlled attention brilliantly illumines the mind, so the lapse from watchfulness and from the sweet invocation of Jesus will darken it completely. All this happens naturally, not in any other way; and you will experience it if you test it out in practice. There is no virtue, least of all this blessed light-generating activity, which cannot be learned from experience."* (St. Hesychios the Priest, in the *Philokalia*)

In Athonite terms, or in the terms of the Early Fathers, worries about all this are based on weakness of faith, and it was on Athos that I first discovered for myself that experience has the power to make changes in us, as well as to inform us. By such experience, one begins, in a consistent way, to understand the changes in other people.

It is this different form of science, *'the knowledge that proves itself by the changes it makes in man,'* that leads to the true *theology of experience*, arising from the tilled earth of practical religion: from the liturgy, from prayer, from bearing one's cross, and spiritual obedience.

This, I suppose, is *theologos*, in the original Greek meaning of the word; it is the icon, the image, the reflection of God in mankind; a theology of and a sharing of personal spiritual experience, in which one understands the words of the Early Fathers not by analysis, but by *recognizing* the things they describe.

This is a science in which truths are recognized not so much through the changes they make in circumstance, as for the changes they make in people.

A different-science leads to different-attitudes, and different-attitudes may lead to a different-society, perhaps even a society a little more like that on Athos.

ENGLAND ONCE KNEW THIS

Once, long ago, as we read in the Venerable Bede, a similar concentration on spirit and a similar austerity of the flesh existed in the monasteries of Britain.

> *"So frugal were Coleman and his predecessors that when they left the seat of their authority there were very few buildings except the church; indeed no more than met the bare requirements of a seemly way of life. They had no property except cattle, and whenever they received any money from rich folk, they immediately gave it to the poor; for they had no need to amass money or to provide lodging for important people, since such visited the church only in order to pray, or to hear the word of God. Whenever opportunity offered, the king himself used to come with only five or six attendants ... But when they happened to remain for a meal, they were content with the plain daily food of the brothers and asked for nothing more.*
>
> *For in those days the sole concern of these teachers was to serve God, not the world; to satisfy the soul, not the belly. Accordingly, the religious habit of that time was held in high esteem ... On Sundays the people flocked to the churches and monasteries, not to obtain food, but to hear the word of God." (Ecclesiastical History of the English People,* by Leo Sherley Price. Penguin Classics, 1990)

ON ATHOS

Mount Athos (MG)

On Athos, then, this same ascetic tradition of early Christianity survives today, which dwelt in far-off Britain, where it was known as the Celtic church, although it was closer to the early Eastern Church.

Indeed, traces of that same art that once flourished on Ireland remain today on Athos: interlaced carvings in stone reminiscent of ancient Irish crosses, and illuminated manuscripts reminiscent of the *Book of Kells*. The Early Fathers of the earliest Greek Church are today the true spiritual ancestors of the hermits. They live by the same rule and in the same great simplicity today in the hermitages of Karoulia, and on many other parts of Mount Athos.

The famous small community of Scetis, once the source to so many inspiring writings, has been the inspiration, too, of modern monastic village communities called *sketes* – larger than the hermit's *kellia* or cell.

These are not only smaller, but often less-formally organized than the twenty great monasteries that rule this sacred mountain. And on the steep slopes of Mount Athos, all of this is dedicated to the spiritual life. So, picturesque as it sounds, Athos is much more than a curiosity. In a sense, the one Athos has two faces: one for the tourist, the connoisseur of art and architecture, who meets the Holy Mountain with eye and camera, backpack and climbing boots.

Some visitors are in such haste to be off again, into those beautiful but rugged paths that link the scattered communities of the mountain, that at dawn they hasten away from the monasteries that have made them so welcome by night. But the more they prove themselves in climbing the *'marble-mountain,'* the less they learn of the greater beauties that live within those ancient walls … and within themselves. Such tourists are of course a problem even for the long-suffering monks of Athos. Constant-interruption has its effect on even the most dedicated life of prayer. So true is this, that the latest of many revivals on Athos owes much to the exodus, within the last thirty years, of complete communities from the pinnacle monasteries of Meteora, where expanding tourism finally drove the most devout monks and nuns away from their refuge of centuries.

Those who love *Panagia's Garden* can only pray that the same does not happen to Athos; that the Spirit that has preserved this unique state for a thousand years can do so today, even in this time of the tourist-trade. Yet even now, the pilgrim finds much less of a welcome in Athos monasteries in September than at the beginning of the year – a phenomenon I have only found in the past in British seaside-resorts, where the late-season guest often finds cold comfort. But there is always another face of the Mountain, one which I suspect Athos shows only to those who love – at least in little – the God she loves so much. That is the face of love and dedication as it exists on so many of a thousand and a half black-clad monks, priest-monks, and hermits who form the main population of this mountain state-within-a-state.

It is these men whose many-hours of prayer, we are told, help to maintain the world. This is one meaning of the idea of Athos as *'the fulcrum of the world.'*

(There are other meanings, too, as anyone knows who has seen, day after day, the multitude of different faces shown by that marble-cone, with its changing expressions as the clouds are parted by its finger, giving rain on one side, and sunshine the other. Athos is a mountain that rarely looks the same from one day to the next.)

So there is scenic Athos, one of many scenic-places, and there is Holy Athos, which is something wholly-unique and very much more than the former. But if we wish to find Holy Athos, then, wittingly or sometimes unwittingly and drawn by some almost unconscious yearning, we must go as a pilgrim. And the essence of pilgrimage is the intention. Going as a pilgrim is not something one can do accidentally. Neither is it easy, especially for those born to our modern all-electric, packaged-civilization. Yet, somehow, this is itself the point of pilgrimage.

What do I mean by this? Simply that the real purpose of Christian pilgrimage is to take a journey to a different part of oneself ... perhaps even to that holy-place where your Saviour lives within you. But here on Athos, change of heart involves sacrifice.

The principle is similar both for monk and pilgrim, as the Abbot of the monastery of Stavronikita on Athos made clear when he wrote recently that: *"'He who loves his life will lose it, but he who hates his life in this world will keep it unto life eternal."* (St. John 2:25)

"The monk, with the total gift of himself to God, saves the one unique truth. He lives the one unique joy. 'He who loses his life in this world, will save it.' The life of a monk is thus a losing and a finding." (Abbot Vasileios of Stavronikita, *Hymn of Entry*)

Not only for monks this is true. For everyone it is true that: *"Every affliction tests our will, showing whether it is inclined to good or evil."* (St. Mark the Ascetic, in the *Philokalia*)

At a lower level, this idea strangely echoed something I had thought some years before, that we had misunderstood evolution: that survival of the fittest, nature-red-in-tooth-and-claw, applied wherever there is lack of attentive, conscious and considerate control.

Man the husbandman can make nature more humane when allowed to, by following the commandment, by attentively doing the will of God, as Father Paisios put it.

Yet Man the exploiter makes nature less-humane, as we also well-know, creating suffering by misuse of power. *"Needs must that scandals come, but woe unto him by whom they come."* (Matthew 18:7)

Man's own life is subject to the same law, that what we do not learn the easy way, by being watchful, *(nepsis),* we learn the hard way, by failure and disaster, *(thlipsis).*

Somehow, there is a link between watchfulness and God-mind-edness, but also another between carelessness and the difficulties that result from it.

"If you worry about the world then you have the world and its problems. If you turn towards God, then it is as the Gospel says: 'Seek first the Kingdom of God, and all else shall be added to you.'

"If you look first to God, you can rely on God to care for you; but of course, to provide what you really need, not what you think you should have." (From Sister A in conversation at the convent of Ormylia)

St. Anthony the Great also spoke of this in a letter, after saying that:

"I think, brethren, that the souls which draw-near to the love of God are of three sorts, be they male or female. The first sort," he said, *"were those who had from their birth a love of God in their hearts. The second were drawn to God from a fear of hellfire."* About the third sort, he said that: *"The third calling is this: There are souls which at first were hard of heart and persisted in the works of sin; and sometimes the good God in his mercy sends upon such souls the chastisement of thlipsis, till they grow weary, and come to their senses, and are converted, and draw near, and enter into knowledge, and repent with all their heart, and they also attain the true manner of life ... "* (Saint Anthony the Great, in the *Philokalia*)

CHAPTER 2

ARRIVAL AT KARYES

As a pilgrim, I had found the need to continue on to the point where the Christian must take up his Cross. At this point we must begin to sacrifice the myriad personal demands we make on life; for me, all the little foibles and habits which make me so secure in my ordinary life: not in the survival sense, but secure to enjoy the standard of living to which I had become accustomed. My difficulties began immediately when I arrived in Karyes, for this was where I had to decide which path to follow of those that spread-out in all directions from the town.

I had heard that even the most important tracks between monasteries were signposted only at major junctions, if there. We had seen the great number of scratches and abrasions collected by Dietrich, a bearded German pilgrim, when he had accidentally left the main track leading from monastery to monastery. It had taken him five and a half hours to reach his destination: it should have been three and a quarter. Another uncertainty! I had no idea whether the tracks were easy or difficult to follow between junctions. (Had I known how much they had deteriorated in recent years, I should have been even more uncertain.) I did not know what time I would be able to start from Karyes, so the sunset 'deadline' was to me much more than an abstract mathematical problem, especially as some of the steep climbs involved had made it unwise for me to attempt to carry much food or any camping gear. Water is no problem. A pint container is enough, as it is easy enough to find water to refill it.

A second alternative was a dirt road from Dafni. This climbed to about twelve-hundred-feet, before descending again to the monastery-entrance at a little over nine-hundred. It was said to take two hours, but it actually took me around three and three-quarters.

The third route initially appeared easiest, on the morning boat from Dafni. But after the easy boat ride would come the payment, a nine hundred foot climb up from the monastery's arsenal by a steep rough stone mule track.

The fourth route was the coast-path from the monastery of Gregoriou, or others further up the peninsula, ending with the same nine hundred foot climb, also steep. I decided not to risk it. Timing is the biggest problem. It was about 10:30 in the morning by the time I regained my passport from the local police-station, in a building which at first appeared to be a ruin, with gaping-windows, and untidy rubble in the ground-floor rooms.

However, closer investigation disclosed a side door, a courtyard, and in the courtyard a staircase – and there was at one time a sign there, saying in English, *'Aliens Police.'* There my passport was returned, and with that and yet another form, I went next to the imposing building of the 'Holy Community,' the headquarters building of the Athos Community of twenty main monasteries – each of them ruling its own feudal domain.

The big doors are up a flight of about twenty-four wide stone steps. Inside the doors is a large hall with doors on either side, and a central staircase. At the far end, in a glassed-in-kiosk tucked back in the shadows under the imposing staircase, was a silent, bespectacled monk, and there I joined the queue to pay for my *Diamonitorion,* the pass that would allow me to actually visit the monasteries.

STRANGENESS OF KARYES

Karyes – Main Square (RA)

31

To the newcomer, Karyes is in many ways the most alien part of Athos. With a little effort, one can feel at home in the monasteries. But in all-male Karyes, in spite of the bus and some other motorized transport, I still feel that one might just as well be in Lhasa, Tibet, or back in the Dark Ages.

There, it is as if the last few centuries had never been. Even so, a little before eleven, I managed to obtain a coke from one of Karyes' two 'hotels' – with a great sound of chattering coming from their gloomy doorways in contrast to the remarkable silence of the little town. Both were truly medieval in character, decor and casualness, except for the bottles of Coca-Cola and Fanta cooling outside in a stone trough of spring-water. Above the spring, by way of surprise, was the same eye at the center-of-the-sun symbol that we had found carved in the stone over the old front door at Weatherall, our house in the 1970's in the Forest of Dean, in far-away England. In summer-time Greece, of course, cooling is all-important. By the time I had completed the paperwork, it would not be long before twelve, (on later visits it was sometimes as late as two), and the temperatures at that time were those in which the locals in that part of Greece normally take siesta from 1 or 2 pm until about 5 pm. Yet after 5 pm, there is little time before sunset and the closing of the monastery doors.

Now that I was ready to move on, it was time I did so, if only I knew where to move on to. But this is where the timing becomes important. Between Dafni and the 'Skete of St. Anne,' at the tip of the peninsula, communication between the monasteries is made easier by a fifty-foot caique that leaves Dafni at two. One-boat-a-day means a need for careful planning. The map I had did not give distances, and the walking-times listed were for me highly optimistic.

Notes provided with my map recommended that one should travel in company in case of accidents. They mentioned snakes, and casually stated that wolves are now rare on the mountain. One monk told me recently of a friend that was treed by wolves for a winter night only a year or two back, but on one of the more remote paths. Of course, one is never quite sure; some Athos monks have quite a sense of humor.

But wild-boar is still hunted there, and I have read reports that hyenas have been seen since the Second World War.

I have also watched eagles rising on the up-drought over the crest. Yet in fact, all I saw on this first trip were a couple of very commonplace small lizards.

But certainly, the journey to the Holy Mountain provides a real icon of the spiritual search with its uncertainties and its need for trust. In fact, my final-decision as to route was dictated by some English-speaking Germans I met in Karyes. They were going directly to Simonos Petra, and were returning to Dafni by bus to make their start. Most uncertain of the overland route, I decided to follow them at least on the 12:30 bus to Dafni, where I would still have several choices.

THLIPSIS

Although I met difficulties on my first visits to Athos, and indeed on every visit, perhaps there was good reason that only on my sixth visit did I learn how much this whole question was a major concern of Orthodox theology. After I left Athos, with my wife I visited a nearby convent, The Holy Monastery of the Annunciation, near the small town of Ormylia, between the Westernmost and middle peninsulas, Cassandra and Sithonia. Athos is the Easternmost.

The convent was under the direction of Simonas Petra monastery. There we had a conversation with one of the sisters about this Greek concept of *thlipsis,* which also contains our contemporary idea of acceptance, the idea that we should not worry too much about externals. This talk, obviously drawing on the sister's experience, as well as on doctrinal ideas, somehow summed up many of the big questions raised by my experiences on Athos, and by the whole patristic tradition. It pointed to the universality of truth in the way it linked the Indian idea of 'giving up' with the philosophical idea that we should 'give up our suffering.' This view puts the Christian idea of sacrifice in a different light.

"Life always has problems," the nun, Sister A, told my wife when we visited her convent after I had been to Athos once again. "In this world we are in exile. You can turn your back on the world as a true exile, a monk or nun.

The monk or nun dies to the world. And when you cut yourself off from the world, you cut off many of the problems. "St. Paul says that 'it is better to marry than to burn.' You can choose to marry, to live in the world with its problems: then the problems are there. There is a word in Greek – thlipsis, it has two meanings. It means grief and affliction, and it means restriction, squeezing, limitation. Thlipsis is the word for this situation in the world: if you choose the world, you have thlipsis.

"Each person's thlipsis is different, right for them, to bring them, in-time, to God. People in the world choose many things for comfort and convenience, and with this comes the need to acquire things and look after things; to think about getting a better house, a job with more money, things like this; from this arise our problems; our thlipsis. The saints of God welcome thlipsis, it stops them forgetting: one saint, when he found life too easy, prayed to God to bring back his thlipsis. If you choose God," she continued, "that is different. That is real choice. In other choices we have no control, no real choice. But not only a monk or nun can choose God, anybody can choose God." So we can be 'in the world, but not of it.' There is an inner-desert, an inner 'monastery-of-the-heart' whose door may open to each one of us.

Thlipsis, then, is itself a part of a mystery. Hidden in it is the 'recipe' for changing the heart, a means of transforming difficulties into something good and positive. This kind of transformation is one of the basic elements of pilgrimage.

Superficially, a pilgrimage is simply a visit to holy-places, perhaps to enjoy the 'atmosphere' found there, perhaps to indulge oneself in the 'shock' of the unfamiliar ... perhaps ... perhaps. Done for their own sake, such things are a self indulgence, a placebo for the divine-discontent that is our birth-right, sugar-coated and 'ingested' to hide from ourselves the lurking awareness that, unless it is done with God, nothing we do has any real significance.

Of course, our normal self-delusions go against the true purpose of pilgrimage. The real value of such a journey of the spirit is found in the search for inner-freedom from ourselves. This freedom we must seek is freedom from the selfishness that comes between ourself and God.

It is not that difficulty is a virtue in itself – it is not – but because what keeps human life bound and limited is our normal unwillingness to overcome certain difficulties. Our modern comforts and conveniences exist with the express-purpose that many of the difficulties proper to human life might be avoided. But then, perhaps, the maturity that these difficulties bring is also avoided.

PAIN & SUFFERING

> *"Mount Athos can help to return to Europe an awareness of what its own, unique contribution among the great civilizations of the world must be, that is: to comprehend the meaning of the human person and of a person-centered society."* (Archimandrite Placide, of the Monastery of Simonas Petra)

The problem of pain and suffering is a strange one. The Athonite answer to it can sometimes seem to trouble modern man. In the West we have failed to find a positive explanation of these things. This is inevitable: to Western, humanist thought, no such explanation is possible, because it belongs to aspects of life which such thought ignores. This is because almost all humanist thought contains an implicit emphasis on the changing by man of man's environment, and not the other way round.

This is an attitude that is inextricably linked with the general lack of faith in our civilization. But with faith comes trust, and he who truly trusts overcomes both fatalism and the attendant attitude of exploitation, so, even where the action is the same, the motivation and hence the quality of the act can be different.

However, on Athos, it seems apparent that the question of suffering is only explainable, and suffering can only be overcome in a universe in which the forces of change are understood to act upon and through man. So much is the latter attitude true of Athos that, on my earliest visits, I discovered as much about myself as about the Holy Mountain. Neither of these was easy: to discover the Athos of the historian, the scholar, the backpacker, is difficult enough. To discover the religious heart of Athos is more difficult. One has to overcome preconceptions as well as physical problems, to cross communication gaps, as well as climb mountains, and to uncover the secrets of one's own heart can be most difficult of all, for the roots of all our difficulties lie there. But on this path of pilgrimage, *thlipsis:* difficulty, has a positive value. The difficulties of pilgrimage are not purely psychological or imaginary, as are many of the problems in Western life. They are both real and revealing.

To begin with, even in this day of airline-travel and packaged-tours, getting to Mount Athos is not easy. The difficulties began early on my first visit to the Holy Mountain. Indeed, they began as soon as I reached Thessaloníki for the first time. This big and bustling modern city must now, after being almost burned to the ground in the Second World War, be very different from when St. Paul taught the Thessalonians all those centuries ago. There, crossing the ancient pathways of St. Paul, in a hotel somewhat worse than it was advertised to be, I passed through an uncomfortable and, I must admit, only temporary adaptation to noise, mosquitoes, and food, in an environment far more alien than appears at first sight. Unless spending a great deal of money, it is at Thessaloníki that the intending visitor to Athos must begin to surrender his preconceptions – and like me, you might discover that some of them are not easily surrendered.

Aristotelous Square, Thessaloninki (RA)

Put dispassionately, Athos challenges and tests the Western approach to life, an attitude based on the idea that we can *do:* that we are the controllers of our lives, the 'actors' in all that we do. This pride of ours is challenged by a world we can never actually control.

To take one example; because of this belief that we are able to 'do' whatever we set out to do, we habitually decide in advance just what we intend – particularly in difficult situations. So much is this a part of our lives that, when it becomes impossible to plan, to predict, or to control, we become frightened. Our whole Western environment is shaped to protect us from this kind of fear: to support our illusion of command.

As a result, I first met this fear at Thessaloníki – where it took us twenty-four difficult hours to obtain approvals from the Ministry and the 'Aliens Police,' with several unnecessary journeys and additional delays because of misinformation, even though my wife speaks passable Greek. Without her, I would have been entirely lost.

Every single-time when we were told what time to call for some piece of paper or other, the time would be wrong. More taxi-journeys would be needed, up to the imposing Ministry of Northern Greece in the higher part of the city, then back down to our hotel nearer the waterfront.

The delays did not end there. Because there is a limit – I soon understood why – for admission of non-Greeks to Athos, it was necessary to wait until the following Sunday, our eighth day in Greece, before I could actually get onto the Mountain, and this was only just sufficient time for us to obtain a minimum of information about travel on the Holy Mountain, and to allow my ankle – swollen to almost twice its usual size by mosquito bites on the first two nights – to reduce to its normal size and usefulness.

KNOWLEDGE OF THE HEART

Underlying the possibility of change of heart is what can be called *'the knowledge of the heart:'* I believe that, in the past, the Greek word for this kind of knowledge was *gnosis*. But over the centuries, this word *gnosis* has been so greatly abused by imitators that it has – perhaps justly – fallen into disrepute. The reason for this, of course, is that the real thing is in general so uncommon that in our memories, substitutions occur.

But in the *Garden of Panagia,* the monastic republic of Athos, something of the quality of those early monks who shaped the church is reflected by today's monks, and especially by the rare *'elder members'* of the Eastern Church – the true *'startsi'* or *'gerontes'* – the *elders*. These elders are the 'professors' of this other kind of knowledge, the researchers in this other science, and its results are shared more in present help than in written description, more in description than explanation. They have little or no equivalent in the Western world, nor in Roman and Protestant churches, for the elder often has no outward status, no rank, and instead, can be totally wrapped in humility. Yet he – or she – is the true theologian, and even those immediately around them would hesitate to claim such a high calling for themselves.

"Theology is such a high thing," said one of my friends on Athos recently, *"that most of us here hesitate to call ourselves theologians."* The elder, the true theologian, has what our modern Western world lacks, while the Western world hoards what the elder has rejected as trivial. So the truth of the heart, the truth of the elder, is not divisible as our truths are, idea from action, theory from practice.

You cannot approach the knowledge learned by the elder without approaching the values held by the elder.

You cannot know what the elder knows, unless you become an elder.

A man I knew and valued had followed up an earlier connection on Mount Athos. He made contact with the monk whose words were described in the typescript mentioned in the first chapter of this book. They had corresponded, but had never met. After that, the English end of the correspondence had died, leaving this possibility unfulfilled, so that I believed there was a danger that for a second time this connection between England and the Holy Mountain would fade. (I was then unaware of the small but constant trickle of pilgrims that visit Athos from England, year after year.) It was at this time that fate seemed to take a hand in true Greek fashion. That year, my wife visited her family home high in the mountains of the Peloponnese.

Talking to a cousin, she discovered that he had been on Athos that year as a contractor for one of the monasteries. Although difficult, access to Athos was far from impossible. The visit to her family home had inspired my wife to see more of the Greece she had never seen before. Would I like to join her on another visit: perhaps to Athos, and perhaps to walk in the footsteps of the Saints?

A DIFFERENT PLACE IN MYSELF

The time was right. The plan was made that was to challenge my deeply ingrained English view of the world: to give me a different view of our ideas, and our assumptions; of our materialism and our science; our linguistic-philosophy, and our rationalism, our self-seeking, our constant niggling dependence one upon the other, and the concern with economics that this entails. But above all, it was to give me a different view of myself. A view from the Mountain, that was also a view-of-myself from a different place in myself.

Much of this different view came from conversations I had with the monks on the Mountain, and from the thoughts stimulated by this wild, silent and beautiful 'Garden of *Panagia*'; from its stillnesses and its wildnesses; from its beauty and its rigors; from the tears of its many pilgrims and the asceticism of its few perceptible hermits; from its unchanging character; from the thoughtlessness of its tourists, and the year-in-year-out dedication of its monks (for Athos, it is said, is still substantially the same today as a thousand years ago).

Above all, it came from the most private experiences, those that all these things generated in the indefinable but living depths of my soul, experiences that are difficult to talk about, yet which have totally changed my life. In beginning, on Mount Athos, to learn about myself in a new and different way, I began also to learn about my humanity in a different way. As I did so, I began to see that what this relic of a plundered Byzantium has to offer us, inwardly blind as we are, is some forgotten insight into ourselves. I learned that not only I, but all of us, our whole civilization, were almost entirely-lacking in even that imperfect self-knowledge which seems to have been normal to earlier civilizations. All of this I had thought before.

But now, as I learned to see the 'view from the Mountain,' I began to think that I might understand what it meant.

WHAT THEN IS PILGRIMAGE?

This is a question of heart, not just of head, nor simply of physical effort. It is, as Father I of Simonos Petra once told me, a journey to a holy place, a place to discover the eternal within oneself. Pilgrimage is a journey into oneself. It is also willing devotion, and it is change enforced by invited circumstance, and willingly accepted.

On the one hand, one intensifies devotion by giving it expression in physical effort, so expressing the unity of spirit and body. On the other, by leaving behind all that is familiar and easy in one's life, one leaves behind, too, all that is habitual and repetitive.

It is as if the pilgrim is able, in spirit, and for the duration of his pilgrimage, to obey Christ's injunction to: *"Go, and sell all that you have."* (Matthew 19:21)

A modern way of looking at it is that on pilgrimage we sacrifice time – Time, the most precious commodity of modern life. When we lack it, we bemoan the fact. When it is 'on our hands,' we try to fill it. But on pilgrimage, by leaving behind all the things we normally use to fill this 'empty time,' we may find time within us for things that have for too long been missing from our life. By making the gift of time, one becomes free of the bonds of time ... and so – I hoped – we learn to control our time. By doing things we find difficult, we break free of the habit of choosing the 'easy way' in everything. Once free of this, we discover that it is this – the habit of taking the easy-way-out – which binds us to repeat the events of our lives with so little change. It is in this way that we overcome our imagined limitations, those which have too often become habitual boundaries to one's life. And so we discover that difficulties, far from limiting our freedom, may actually increase it.

By sacrificing time, we gain freedom from ourselves. But to discover this, we have to step outside the surprisingly narrow bounds of modern thought and action, to step without hesitation onto the pilgrim's road, accepting the difficulties of unfamiliar conditions as we more easily accept new ideas. The essence of pilgrimage, then, is giving-up. One gives-up the ordinary for the extraordinary, the everyday for God, but not as a 'bargain' from which one expects a return.

God, reported the Desert Fathers of old, makes no bargains.

So one gives-up oneself in order to know a better self, or simply in order to prove, in one's own flesh, to one's own self, the reality of one's commitment to something higher than oneself. For example, habits are difficult to overcome. They are easily begun, but once begun, they become difficult to see, and almost impossible to remedy. But one idea of pilgrimage is the 'friction struggle' against our habits. This begins when we place ourselves in a position where our habits no longer provide solutions, where they are not acceptable, not appropriate. It is in such circumstances, I found, that many of our habits and attitudes become suddenly visible to us!

RECOGNITION-KNOWLEDGE

Here it is helpful to understand *recognition* as a little-understood form of knowledge of the heart; one which is not part of our education, and which is rarely perceived by people at the present time. When we perceive it, this changes our whole conception both of knowledge and of religion. Even before this, as one begins to study Athos, one first discovers, at the very least, that here there is something very close to the Desert-Fathers of fifteen hundred years ago. The heart, in the sense used by the Fathers, has knowledge of an entirely different kind from that of the intellect. The heart obtains knowledge of a kind which, once-gained, may never be changed. Forgotten today, this is the kind of knowledge that formed the 'unwritten' traditions of the past, and which remains the basis of the true 'patristic' Christian tradition today.

Indeed, the whole concept of change of heart needs to be understood better, although it can never be easily explained, because it touches on what we call 'mysteries.' But if the concept of change of heart cannot be easily explained, it can be *recognized*.

The key to the whole question of spiritual-knowledge lies in this fact, that certain things happen in human life that we cannot explain even today, even with all our knowledge, yet we can *recognize* them. But to recognize something is to know it, although with a knowledge quite different from the 'explanatory' knowledge of modern science, which is drawn from other men's words, and finds its evidence in the limited vista presented by the five senses.

Continuity and agreement are the visible signs of this emotional *recognition knowledge.*

The first signs I found that there on Athos they maintain this continuity, and remember this long ago past, were in the way the monks reverence their own dead. They follow an old tradition (a better word in this case might be 'custom') of digging up the bones after a few years, then storing them in a charnel house, where they remain as mute evidence of generations of monks that have gone before them. Over this vault they build a chapel, and put much time and love into that chapel.

This not only demonstrates the love of disciple for disciple of which Christ spoke, but it also reveals, in stillness and in joy, the original strength of Christian attitudes to death, seen by them as a true entry into heaven. The future which in-part has already been revealed to them in the liturgy.

This visible continuity is one reason why, in making the trip to Athos, one finds oneself making an enormous leap back into the past of the Christian faith. The voices are surely the same. The ideas are surely the same. The methods are almost certainly little changed. The words of the services are the same: the main liturgy each day still follows the form laid down by St. John Chrysostom in the third century.

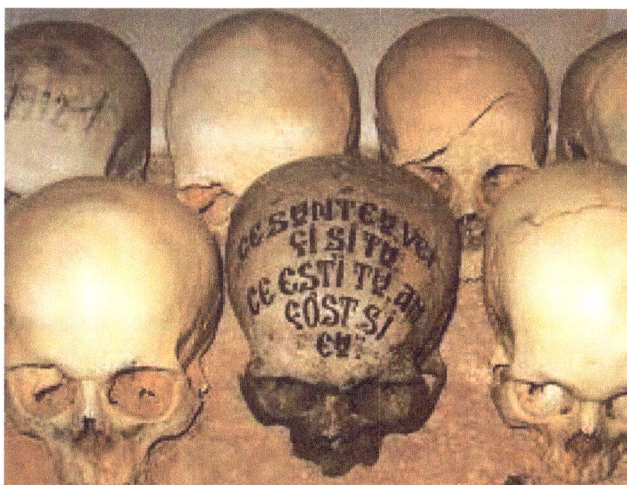

Ossuary, Athos (adriatikus)

CHAPTER 3

A PILGRIM'S PROBLEMS

Garden of *Panagia* (MG)

To understand the pilgrim's view of Athos, one must first understand certain things about the Holy Mountain. Athos is a land of puzzles, many of which arise out of problems. Typical of these are events that lie on the borderline of coincidence. A German film-producer tells how, walking the paths of Athos, hot from the vertical sun, he passed an orange tree beside a ruined hermit's cell. There were many ripe oranges on the tree, but all out of reach, so he prayed to the dead hermit that an orange would fall to him. Nothing-happened. After resting, he continued on his way. Some time later, he arrived on the quayside at Dafni just as the boat arrived. As usual at this time, the quayside was crowded with many monks and pilgrims, all waiting for the bus or boat. As he approached this crowd, a priest emerged, a total stranger to him, and handed him an orange.

How does one interpret such events? Not with blind faith so much as with uncertainty. It is in this uncertainty, this openness, that the pilgrim first begins to understand the monk. As you accept your situation and give up your self into the hands of God, you begin to die to the old, the false self, and so become a little more monk-like. As you become monk-like in your attitude, and this is sensed by the monks, you become able to enter their world and their hearts, receive their friendship, and visit their monasteries by invitation. By this, Athos becomes transformed from what is already a place of beauty, of mystery, and of history, to something more: for you, too, it is now the Garden of *Panagia*, the Virgin's garden, on the mountain of God's peace.

The Virgin's garden is the all-holy garden. This garden paradise is of course an ancient image of the human soul. It is familiar from Genesis. It occurs in the Koran. The masters of the Quabalah developed it with great complexity. Today the yogis of India speak of the human organism as containing some '*antakharana*' in which exist the seeds of all human possibilities. In different people, different seeds germinate, and as they do so, they create different problems, or sometimes different strengths, the talents given us by God. When the talents grow, they can combine to form part of a greater growth. "*Blessed are the pure in heart.*" (Matthew 5:8)

The Garden of *Panagia* is this garden transformed. In the Garden of *Panagia,* the true fruit is the Son of God: the birth of Christ in the human heart.

IMPORTANCE OF TRUST

The greatest puzzles of Athos lie in the need to trust. Not to trust somebody in the flesh, but to trust God, to trust things as they are, and so, above all, to trust ourselves, for as St. John said, '*we are given power to become sons of God*' (John 1: 12-13).

Though we live in comfortable times, it isn't just our comfort we must sacrifice. What turned my visit to Athos from holiday to pilgrimage was the way things made me sacrifice all my control over circumstance, all the little foibles and habits which had made me so secure in my ordinary life: not only in the survival sense.

This also affected the security of my personal way of life. On Athos, many things combined to separate me from this accustomed security: the circumstances where I did not understand the difficulty of communicating. There, the most important factor of all is the living faith of the monks, who will not make anything rigid, lest they prevent God from making things happen. All my planning for my own comfort must be forgotten, and I must, from the very moment I set foot on that holy-shore, be prepared to find that my hand had been gently removed from the rudder of my life, so that I, with all my needs and all my weaknesses, was powerless in the hands of God. But is this not the real sacrifice of pilgrimage, to place oneself willingly in God's hands, with the purpose of purposelessness: with commitment, but with no rigid plan?

But for the newcomer to Athos, I discovered, there are certain things without which this transformation of attitude is impossible: the sanctity that rules over Athos gives a certain freedom. Its atmosphere of peace soaks into the pilgrim's heart. The recognizable efforts made by its monks provide a model to be imitated. And the visitor is sensitized to all these things by the unfamiliarity of Athos, a world more different than one can easily imagine, simply because its people live-differently.

Because of this, beginning from my first visit, all the information I had collected had been entirely inadequate to prepare me for the reality, so inadequate that not only could I not plan my itinerary in advance, I was not even certain of my own physical capabilities under such unfamiliar conditions.

DOWN THE MOUNTAIN

The bus-journey up the mountain from Dafni to Karyes was nerve-wracking enough. The journey down was worse. As the oldest bus I had seen in Greece groaned and bumped its way down the rocky and precipitous road, the driver kept up an excitable conversation with a number of locals sitting behind him, pausing occasionally to glance at the road ahead, where the wheels seemed to pass within inches of the void, an edge that, so often in Athos, overhung either deep ravines or the steep slopes to the blue Aegean below.

The extra adrenaline this aroused etched many things in my mind: especially the untidy order of the monastery of Xeropotamou, a monastery so old that nobody can agree when it was started, or by whom. As we zigzagged towards the sea below, Xeropotamou was first seen far beneath us on the mountain, then glimpsed through old olive trees as we stopped beside the monastery to let off passengers. Xeropotamou looks to the visitor like some enormous, millennia-old castle, but with balconies instead of battlements. It rises from a flat area of fields and groves, half-way-up the southern ridge of Athos.

It was last seen rising through the trees far above us, as the bus accelerated down the final slope into the little port of Dafni; viewed as rooftops from far above. Then there was a stop where a joking monk held up the bus for several minutes by refusing to allow the door to be shut. As he let go, the gray-bearded monk sitting beside me crossed himself.

Finally, about one-fifteen, we reached Dafni, once again with no information except that the caique was ready to depart up the coast to the arsanas of Simonos Petra, to the almost sea-level monastery of Gregoriou, then to the cloister of St. Dionisious, another monastery built on a high rock, and beyond, to the monastery of Saint Paul, and then to the so-called New *Skete* and on to the *Skete* of St. Anne. (These smaller dependencies or *metochi* of the main-monasteries, are named, as I said earlier, after the early African community at Scetis. They follow a stricter regime than the monasteries.)

Forty-five minutes before the boat left, most of my fellow-travelers went to the taverna on the quayside. I saw them a few minutes later, drinking minerals at the gray wooden tables under a truly ancient wisteria, its trunk more than a foot across, which shades the front of the cafe. It was only then that I finally decided my route. I would begin with the walk to Simonos Petra. I didn't know how far that would be. The height was more than the straight climb, because one goes up some way above the monastery – then 'down' again, at 1000 feet or so. (To think I used to consider the climb (by car) from the Severn Bridge to the Forest of Dean to be a serious climb ... from two hundred feet to seven hundred or so!)

My associates would be going by boat, then taking the straight thousand-foot climb up to the monastery. (Even my Greek guide-book labels it *'tiring climb'*). At least if I miscalculated the time, they could tell people there was still someone on the road. So I told them I was going to walk, and simply set-off.

The track was wide, safe, and easy to follow. Round the corner was a typical Athos sight, several rough staffs lying by the ditch. I took-up one of them, and continued past some timber-yards.

The time element was and still is for me one of the big 'hurdles,' as it must be for many visitors when they first come to Athos. There was no doubt about it, if I was to benefit from the introductory letter to Simonos Petra, which chance and my wife's telephone calls had brought me, I had best reach there on that first day. But on foot, Simonos Petra may be the most inaccessible monastery on all of Athos. Although approachable by four routes, it stands high above the sea which is often the easiest thoroughfare from monastery to monastery. One of the routes was a hard-to-locate track from Karyes, winding along the ridge of the peninsula and reported as normally a four-and-a-half hour walk – but I did not have my mountain-legs yet, and even if I did not lose the way, there were only between six and seven hours before the doors would be shut for the night. I decided not to risk this. Experience soon proved this decision correct.

WALK FROM DAFNI

Passing behind the big stone buildings around the timber-yard at Dafni, the rough-road crossed a stream. Then it began its slow climb up the lower slopes of the mountain. Soon, it seemed, the sea was far below. Less than thirty minutes later, when the boat started, it seemed really tiny, so far below, on the gray water of the gulf across to the next peninsula, distant Sithonia.

Athos, on its South West side, is a series of small mountains divided by ravines. At the bottom of each ravine a dried stream-bed was filled with boulders. Cliffs down to the sea, and the often cliff-like sides of the ravines, determine the zigzag routes taken by the coastal tracks.

Wooded path on Athos (MG)

There is no straight-route, man goes wherever he can, on the safest slope above the cliffs; zigzagging up headlands; through woodlands; over rocks; following the contour up the side of a ravine; until he reaches a place where the slope is gradual enough to allow him to descend to the stream bed. Then, soon, he must climb again to continue the process. The road from Dafni did the same, a little more gently.

In places, the road had visibly been blasted from the hillside to meet the needs of modern transport, so everywhere there were rocks blasted or bulldozed from the earth. In one place one walked on marble, in another, on sand or crumbling mica. For someone who for years had done his climbing in the driving seat of a car, it was a new world. Discovering how to pace myself for the climb, I was learning much about myself, a self as strange as the unfamiliar mountain land. As the road rose around the first big headland, I found the need to overrule my established walking habits, and settled to a slower but steadier pace.

On the south side of the peninsula, the midday-sun came straight in, its angle to the bulldozed-road changing slightly as it wove its way amongst the trees. I learned to stop at every decent patch of shade I could find. Rocks, scrappy oaks, and sometimes acacias, provided rare islands of roadside shelter. The vegetation itself was often familiar. Spanish chestnut and small conifers abounded. Occasional wild-figs must have provided some nourishment to travelers, but I saw no ripe fruit, evidence that travelers were not uncommon. Heather was common, and an abundance of broom took the place of the gorse that dominates similar ground in Britain.

Soon the first hour had passed. On my map, the journey divided into three main sections. I was still on the first of them, the climb from Dafni that swung around a headland, so that it was difficult to judge how far I had gone, how far I had yet to go. Then was the second-section, a zigzag along the side of a ravine to join another road coming from above. That junction was the highest point on my route. The occasional patch of shade allowed me barely enough energy to continue. Still, the route continued much the same, weaving along, passing behind a rock, then and returning again to the sea. One-and-a-half-hours had passed before I was sure I had reached the second-section of the route, a zig-zag climb. At the end of this, I had gone roughly half-way in horizontal terms, but the worst of the climbing was behind me. Now, I was moving away from the sea. Below me, the ravine; above me, occasional great outcrops and pinnacles of rock. On the road beside me, an occasional footprint in the dust.

An oral Tradition

On Athos, the idea of '*paradocis*' is more complex and more meaningful than its Western translation as 'tradition,' with its many meanings. Certainly, it means a great deal more than a set of rules or fixed-beliefs. In English, we have no single word that now conveys its full meaning. I began to glimpse the problem of changing concepts on my first visit to the mountain. When I arrived at Simonos Petra, I spoke to Father I, who agreed to meet me that evening.

When the time came, he obtained the key for the reception room to one side of the Guest Hall. There, in Victorian rather than Byzantine splendor, on long benches covered with almost equally long cushions upholstered in golden yellow, surrounded by ornate 19th century chairs painted a light brown so that in the dim light they looked polished, and in a room with its walls hung with photographs of past abbots and other notables, we had our first conversation.

Although part of the Community, in the typical black robes of an Athos monk, Father I was English. He had originally been intended for the Anglican Church, he told me, but had come to Orthodoxy because he felt more at home with the spiritual and contemplative aspects of that religion.

Also, he liked its orthodoxy. *"Tradition,"* he said, *"it is necessary to have tradition."* Athonite monks see themselves as keepers of this *'paradocis.'* Part of this is that they believe – or actually understand – that truth does not change, and so it does not have to be reinvented, even though it may be restated. This attitude to the preservation of traditional truth goes back long before the time of St. Simon the Athonite, who founded the monastery in the 13th Century

On Athos, they preserve this early truth unchanged. One way this is done is by the way they put it into practice – continuous practice that ensures that the original meaning is not easily forgotten. They also preserve it in writing, sometimes translating or explaining the Early Fathers to make their knowledge available in different languages. The recently published translations of the *Philokalia* into English were suggested by Athonite monks. This idea of a 'received' or 'given' tradition, which is found in many faiths, and so strongly represented on Athos, links with two things which puzzled me early-on about life on the Holy Mountain. One is that there seems to be quite remarkably close agreement between the monks about what they believe, yet they show all the signs of having minds of their own.

This then links with the earlier meaning of the Latin word *educare*, which originally expressed a process of 'drawing truth out' of the student, not 'knocking it in.'

So this is probably the closest you will find today to the forgotten form of the early Church: a Church whose theology is still tested continually against actual practice, even today. This care seems to be how they preserve the last survival, as one might describe it, of the practice of Christianity in its original form. Here is the true inner-desert of the mind; here they still respect and practice the ancient psychology of the Fathers, those early saints whose inner-experience, which was based on deep-knowledge of human nature, remains as effective today as it was two thousand years ago.

Here, even those whose lives dictate a different approach, a different way of life from the monastic, may find the help we need to interpret the Gospel truths correctly; to understand them, and, in understanding, to grow. For are we not all human? Our very humanity is the soil of that garden we seek to till, but this I will try to explain later, for that help in interpretation is found in the existence of an unbroken oral Tradition.

This *paradocis* is founded on monastic practice so that it transmits to the present day the exact meaning of the message of the Early Fathers.

ACROSS THE RAVINE

This was the most-difficult stretch. The climb up the side of the ravine seemed to go on for an age. England, and our easy way of life, seemed far away ... our English-concerns seemed increasingly trivial. They had nothing to do with the necessities of life on the Mountain; how to get to one's destination before the gates closed; how to discover the shade which was so difficult to find. I began to see how, to a peasant or to one of the desert-fathers, with their simple concerns, it would seem as if our minds revolved constantly, returning time-and-again to our many possessions, and to our strangely-artificial roles in life.

At this point, indeed, I became too involved in my own efforts, and so I ceased to notice much of what glimpses assured me was some very magnificent wild countryside. Then, in the middle of that silence, I heard a vehicle. In all that time, nearly two hours, I had passed nobody, walking or riding.

Now, as I turned onto the next stretch of the zigzag, someone was coming. Below me, the mountain ran down hundreds of feet to the sea.

On both sides of the ravine, it rose another seven or eight hundred feet, but where were the summits of these lower foothills of Athos? The ravine continued. The temptation was to stop and seek a lift, whichever way the vehicle was coming. Instead, I continued to seek a shady-spot in which to stop. As I did so, the noise seemed to come no nearer. I stopped, rested a few minutes, and decided to continue on again.

Within minutes, the road turned another corner, and there I was, on a junction with the inland road; there were small red enamel signs: 'DAFNI,' said one, 'M.SIMONOS PETRA' the other, in both Greek and English lettering. The approaching-engine by now sounded a little closer. I could hear gears changing as the driver negotiated one of the many tight bends. I sat on a rock under trees by that junction, and waited. Finally, he came round the bend on the inland 'arm' of the road, a big, battered truck with hydraulic loading-arm, piled high with the five-inch-diameter tree-trunks that appear to be the staple crop of Greek forests, and driven by a young man in a black shirt.

So dusty was the windscreen, and so high the window, that I cannot say much more about him, but he passed on, down to the timber-yard at Dafni, and I turned towards Simonos Petra, having reached a level road at last.

Now the going was easier, though with little shade. Then the road went into a ravine, and turned steeply up the other side. I stopped for another rest. Next, the road turned downhill around the mountain. Here I met my first walker, a young man in a blue shirt, carrying nothing but a plastic carrier. He nodded and went on. Still the sun came in from the sea. Still the scrubby small trees, occasional patches of olives, with telephone wires following the road, except when they swooped across on the shorter path of the swallow. Then a ravine with a concrete bridge where it turned outward toward the sea again.

After this, I found yet another climb, on which I was easily over-taken by a young monk who – for all his voluminous black robes – passed me and was out of sight in a few minutes.

I was once-again walking down a slope where the curves were shorter, but the mountain ran-away hundreds of feet below. I found shade, and again drank some of my quickly-vanishing water.

The bends in the road were interminable. Symbolically, one anticipates arrival many times before actually rounding that final bend. But I finally did come round one of them and saw, through late afternoon mists, the strangest clouds ever. It was only after walking round yet another big bend that I realized that these odd clouds were not just clouds, but the dimly visible peak of Mount Athos itself, which, at 6,300 feet, was far above the smaller moun-tains over which I walked.

From there, the journey was easier. Round the next bend, the mountain road opened into a wider valley, and in front of me, rooted like a tree on a stumpy-pinnacle of stone which rose sheer from the steep slopes above the sea, was the monastery that was my goal, Simonos Petra, the Rock. As I approached the monastery, the signs of human occupancy became more visible. Beside the road were crude seats of planks on stones. I passed a small dwelling, part cave, part house, with a tiny plot of garden above it.

This was St. Simon's hermitage, built before the monastery. Then another house. In front of me, the monastery itself was cov-ered with level after level of scaffolding, obscuring the balconies that are such a feature of the building.

SYNERGIA

From the sea at least, Simonos Petra seems the most inaccessible monastery on all of Athos. Although approachable by four routes, it is high above the sea, which is the more usual thoroughfare from monastery to monastery.

Monastery of Simonos Petras (en.wikipedia.org)

But every time I have gone to the mountain as pilgrim rather than as tourist, I have found the need to face things that I would normally avoid, to continue-on where I would normally turn back. Every time I do this, I learn more about myself, and even about the spiritual significance of the world.

We must sacrifice the personal demands we make on life. We must accept our *thlipsis*, which is the key to pilgrimage and to the Athonite life.

And early in the Orthodox liturgy, one can hear the phrase: *"It is time for the Lord to act."*

For a long time, this puzzled me. It seemed to me from my rudimentary knowledge that such a statement was 'tempting or testing God,' in the sense meant by the Gospel statement that: *"Thou shalt not tempt the Lord thy God."* (Matthew 4: 7) Finally, I realized that this was information telling the congregation that the liturgy had no meaning in itself but only in man's belief.

When Jesus said: *"Not everyone that saith unto Me, 'Lord, Lord' shall be saved, but he that doeth the will of My Father that is in heaven."* (Matthew 7:21.) ... then Athos links this with the idea of a synergetic relation between God and man, in which we must attempt to pray, to be pure of heart, in order to enter communion, but at the same time we must realize that to do so is impossible without *synergia*: that we cannot achieve these things on our own.

Yet, that what is impossible to Man is possible when God is with us. *Synergia* is synergy: co-operation between God and man.

Synergia is not a simple concept involving some bondage of the mind, but a liberation found in the service of Him *"whose service is perfect freedom."* (Anglican Book of Common Prayer)

The basic idea behind this is that we must become more ourselves, in order to become more what God would have us be. In order to cooperate more fully, we must become more inwardly mature.

Reaching the tunnel-like entrance to the monastery of Simonos Petra, I went in and up the sloping passage, paved with a more carefully constructed version of the typical Athos mule-track: rough stone slabs placed across it every three or four feet. The tunnel continued up, past storerooms, and in one place a low arched chamber that was obviously nearing the end of extensive reconstruction. Finally, I came to a doorway which opened into the small central courtyard of the monastery. There were buildings all round, with arches to the outside balconies, and then, looking around, I found myself looking down over a railing onto a sheer four-hundred-foot drop.

It was only then that I discovered that this yard was not at the base of the monastery, but one-story below the top. On this level were the *Katholikon*, (the monastery church), a refectory, some storerooms, and other buildings whose purpose I never learned, as the monks are not great ones for showing tourists around. Up the flimsy wooden staircase, there was guest-accommodation.

Before I reached the guest-house, I saw again that young monk who had passed me earlier in the afternoon, walking so fast. Now he was leaving the monastery again, saying goodbye to one of the resident monks with much evidence of mutual affection.

His companion caught sight of me, the strange face in the yard, and with a final farewell, turned towards me. There was no doubt of the welcome given by this young monk to the stranger on his threshold. He positively beamed with happiness, clasped me by the hand, and led me to the stairs and the guest-house. In halting English, he asked me if I wished to stay overnight, then guided me to the balcony hundreds of feet above the steeply terraced ground below.

This balcony was a welcome of a different order. Although in time I learned – as they say – to trust it, at first sight, one would normally be doubtful about trusting it ten feet above ground, never mind several-hundred. The floorboards seemed loose. Some of the nails were pried up The crossbeams at the base of the guardrail had been so eaten away that they had great cavities, like a rotten branch that has lain long on the forest floor. That first evening, I stayed nervously far from that edge. My guide disappeared. A few minutes later he reappeared, bearing a tray with a glass of raqi, a plastic jug of clear cold water and a saucer with a large piece of Turkish delight. He invited me to refresh myself. I did, sipping the raqi from the small glass, and washing it down with liberal glasses of water.

Athos Balcony (RA)

CHAPTER 4

WHERE ETERNITY TOUCHES THE EARTH

Mount Athos (MG Christis)

On an early visit to the Mountain, Father I was talking to me about why it is important to some people that they come to Athos: *"There are some places in this world,"* he told me, as we sat on the frail wooden balcony overlooking the sea far below, *"where eternity has touched the earth, where things of eternal significance have happened, and some sense of this remains. Athos is one of these places. By coming here, some people are able to re-establish contact with the eternal element within themselves."*

This is just one aspect of *becoming* oneself, which is so important to the practice of religion in the Athonite sense. *Becoming* is important more in an inward than an external sense.

When they talk about the fact that in some places one can more easily reestablish contact with the eternal, this is important because it is only in awareness of this eternal factor within-us that the mind can rest and become still.

Here, at the center of one's being, one finds Christ. Here lies truth, and here open the doors of love.

This 'place' is perhaps the least-known and least understood key to Athonite psychology. It reflects the gospel image of the *'strait gate,'* the *'eye of the needle,'* yet it also explains the parable of the talents. Understand this, and one understands so much else. Find this, and one finds how to put-into-practice so many ideas which otherwise remain mere theory. Carry out the instructions of the *geron* with sufficient care, and it is this 'place' one comes to. Sometimes I think that only in this intangible place does one become what one is – not an imitation of someone else, but oneself ... becomes wholehearted by refusing to compromise; becomes true by not being economical with the truth; becomes whole by not escaping from emptiness into distraction; by giving, not demanding; by perceiving with care instead of jumping to conclusions.

AN ATHOS WELCOME

But to get back to my earlier account, my climb had given me a tremendous thirst, and now I met the traditional Athos welcome. At one time, this included water, loukoumi, a biscuit and coffee. Of the four, the water is most important, and I must have drunk about three pints in the next couple of hours, simply to make up losses en-route. But this, too, was the situation that enabled me to acquire the taste for raqi at the first glass. Now, today, I am told, the traditional-welcome varies a little from monastery to monastery, but it is always waiting for the traveler, and always most welcome.

It was then that I showed my *diamonitirion,* filled in the visitors-book, and handed over my introductory letter so kindly provided. There, drinking my raqi-and water, I again met one of the people I had left at Dafni waiting for the boat. He had arrived only forty-minutes ago, he told me. His friends were still down by the jetty, swimming.

"They don't know what a climb they have to come," he told me, looking over the balcony at the figures like ants far below. We smiled at the thought.

The balcony of Simonos Petra is, I think, higher above the sea than any skyscraper ever-built. I sat there, on the blue-painted settle, trying not to hear a noisy, bearded tourist who insisted on talking perpetually to everyone in sight. Ignoring his chatter, I watched a leisurely pigeon crossing the terraced olive-groves below, and swallows mobbing a hawk 2300 feet beneath me. There I could look out at a pair of fishing boats, droning slowly along the sea, their movement appearing almost motionless from this height. They came from far-away, I learned, to fish the teeming-waters at the foot of the Holy Mountain.

From the left-hand end of the balcony, I looked up, over the 3,000 foot sister-mountain to the sharp fang of Athos itself, piercing the clear sky, and hiding itself in streamers of mist; a splendid way to develop vertigo or to still the mind in awe at the grandeur of it all.

Next, I was shown to a small, airy dormitory with six creaky but otherwise comfortable beds. (Creaky beds seem to be the rule on Athos.) I washed and changed, then returned in time to be shown into a small side-room where a meal was waiting for we two recent arrivals: my first and best meal on Athos: two smoked fish, slices of buttered potato, salad, and a good bunch of grapes, all rounded-off with a big jug of cold water.

As we were slowly and comfortably finishing our meal, a tall monk came into the room, introduced himself, and said that if I would like to talk, he would see me when I had finished eating. This was my first meeting with Father I.

CHRISTIANITY REMEMBERED

Even the results of this way of life, when one becomes clearly aware of them, seem to be the same as those described by the Early Fathers from the first centuries of the Church in Greece. The more you see of Athos, the more certain it seems that the forms of early Christianity are remembered here in a way no longer recognized in the West, and here, more than just the forms are remembered.

It is written that one does not gather figs of thistles. Continuity is identity.

"The spiritual," said Emerson, *"is that which is its own proof."*

"Atman, the spirit," teaches one of the main traditions of Yoga, *"illumines everything, and can even illumine itself."*

Although there can be disagreement in theoretical theology, there should be little disagreement in a theology based on experience. But even so, no everyday experience can wholly explain this Athonite unity-of-character over the ages! No theory is enough for this kind of thing. The theology of Athos is a theology of direct spiritual and mystical experience, a theology of light-seeing-light, confirming the insight that theology once meant not *'theory about God,'* but *'Theosis, the luminous experiential knowledge of God.'*

There is a certain practical significance to this, which cannot easily be put in writing, but is of great importance to the Christian whose aim is to grow closer to God. As the Divine is not simply and directly describable, there can be neither easily-demonstrable, nor dialectical proof that 'all is being.' The only proof that exists is that which is 'given' to us: and this, says tradition, is given from the Creator to the individual creature. As this is not repeatable, it appears to be *'unscientific.'* As a result, this fact is often forgotten. In our desire for a certainty which we can justify to anyone, and our demand for a *'guaranteed return'* on both time and money invested, we have lost our understanding of self-revealing proof – and without the certainty this revelation gives, we remain incomplete as human beings, unable to understand or accept or trust some essential part of ourselves.

The problem lies in the fact that our thought is based on an assumption, on a myth, or on a habitual demand for control over our own lives. For what we cannot control, we cannot repeat to order. *"The fault lies not in our stars, but in ourselves that we are underlings."* (William Shakespeare, *Julius Caesar*)

In our current civilization, we believe that we, as individuals, can change things. That is to say, we grow up believing that we have a degree of control. We judge one another on this assumption, and so judge harshly.

Yet for me, my every experience of Mount Athos has challenged this belief, and has done so through every aspect of its strange, rugged, and beautiful way of life.

THEOLOGICAL TRADITION

Beware the dangers of misinterpretation of language. *Theologia*, the true Athonite theology, which leads to knowledge of God, is taught indirectly by means of *paradocis* in the form of a Tradition of practice and information that guides the interpretation of the more difficult concepts of the Gospels and the Early Fathers. This can only be properly understood *experientially*.

On Athos, the trap of misinterpretation is a constant danger, due to the greater flexibility and 'generacy' of their language of mythology, the organic language of the ancients, the language of Genesis. In this language, one very valuable image is that of the garden: Adam in the garden, and perhaps paradoxically, the garden as the seedbed in man, the soil I referred to earlier on which: *"a sower went forth to sow."* (Luke 8:5)

This image seems to appear all over the world, always, it seems, with the same underlying meaning. In the Genesis version, man is described as having been expelled from a garden. In Jewish mythology, Adam was described as trying to return to this garden; this *'pardes,'* paradise. Christian tradition retains this idea, not only as an idea, but also as a form of inner-experience. As the abbot of one of the Athos monasteries once said: *"To be in the liturgy is to experience paradise."*

This is true; for in Athonite liturgy, we again capture the tears and the joys of that garden lost to us, which yet lies all around us: the paradise which the head can never perceive unaided by the heart, for this paradise is approached through tears, through self-doubt, through the penetrating experience of repentance ... but never merely through doctrinal ideas, nor simple theory.

It is always an emotional experience, sharp, embarrassing, remorseful, self-revealing, suddenly joyful, often painful, bearing strange undercurrents of sorrow perhaps, but real ... above all, real; the tears of real people.

"Out of the strong came forth sweetness." (Judges 14:14)

This is a kind of psychology, perhaps, but a very different kind from the clinical detachment of much of today's medical-psychology. The scalpel of the mind is turned end for end, and searches into one's own heart, and this – and only this – is *personal theology*, the theology that leads to change. Impersonal theories are blind to its richness.

PARADISE MYTH

Primitive in feeling, the whole paradise-myth yet evokes a strange sense that it is meaningful to us even today. Yet there is one interpretation that could be regarded as fanciful but for a few well-hidden clues, and this is the interpretation that regards the miracles as a garden in which grow Christian flowers, the *'good soil,'* in which the seed of Christian myth that is more than myth – the seed of that sower who *'went forth to sow'* – takes root and may grow: *"First the blade, and then the ear, and then the full corn in the ear."* (Mark 4:28)

One cannot say, perhaps, that we are sure that this interpretation is the original meaning, yet it makes us aware of the possibilities, although the language of mythology should never be taken in a literal way. We can, I think, say that this myth of the garden can express things which cannot be said easily in any other way: things beyond the range of logic, yet more true than any theory. In one sense, this garden exists within man, in the heart, in the soul or psyche, perhaps.

Perhaps the most interesting thing is that in practice, this myth can be interpreted in so many ways, and that these are not only surprising in their depth, but fascinating in the way they fit-together, so that they seem to present a complete picture. As I would paint it, this picture begins with a contradictory image of the garden as a strangely primitive world.

On the one hand, the natural world as it is; the most beautiful of all, unspoiled but 'unimproved,' without protection, without entertainment, without the benefits of human society, or of human mutual support: a place of exile; of forced-independence; the bleak-and-empty-place in which man finds himself whenever he is separated from all the distractions and protections of modern life.

This sounds fanciful, yet we are often separated from such a world only by thin cotton, or by an eight-ounce glass pane. Those who have been there will know of what I speak. Here, then, is the true *pardes*: here the garden, in which human nature grows to the full as a true child of organic life. All this has very precise meaning.

THE TRUE PARDES

The second important aspect of this story is this question of the *Tree of Knowledge of Good and Evil*, and its relation to *'otz chim'*; the *Tree of Life* which – according to Jewish mythology – grew in the *pardes*. To put this simplistically, it tells us that our verbal knowledge obscures life. In some way, just as many people suggest, the two things find themselves in competition, yet this myth does in fact put the record straight. It is not – as so many people suggest – that knowledge is itself harmful: it is the type of knowledge, and the way we react to verbal knowledge when we are not clear about the related experience; this is what does the damage, preventing the growth of the emotional strength proper to man *'in the garden.'*

Again, all this imagery, and the ideas it expresses, would appear fanciful if there were no support for it in fact. As it is, within the borders of Greece the whole small nation of Athos is dedicated to overcoming the wrong use of knowledge, as are other smaller communities here and there around the world. Here, on the Holy Mountain, all these dedicated communities are monastic, the whole nation is this tiny monastic republic of Mount Athos, which I was then visiting. Here, as a last relic of the forgotten Byzantine empire, and of an earlier Christianity. Here, even today, they follow the rules and precepts of the Desert Fathers, the saints who began the Christian monastic life more than two thousand years ago.

That ancient event was an attempt to protect and preserve the original European form of Christianity: one that already began to be forgotten at the time when Constantine adopted Christianity as the established religion of the Eastern Roman Empire.

It was then that the mixing of politics with religion began, that mind-mixing that continues to confuse and plague the Christian world up to the present time.

COMMON LIFE

On Athos, even in the *coenobitic* or 'common life' monasteries, there is little behavioral uniformity outside the actual services. Instead, after their initial formation, there are great differences in character and activity from monk to monk.

The monks show a great deal of initiative, except that, about many things, they refer automatically to their seniors, or to the community at large, and about many things which concern the community as a whole, they often will not make an 'off-the-cuff' decision. I finally began to understand that the Athonite view of tradition links with the idea of the *geron:* the elder monk or man of experience, often the *hegumen* or abbot of a monastery. He is the source of tradition, not in the form of verbal knowledge, but in what he is, in what he has become.

This means that the continuity of Athos is Christian in the sense that it is itself a sign of truth-made-flesh. Moreover, after a thousand years, and with monks coming from different countries, the services are still very close to the original in form and spirit. Even the results on the pilgrim, when one finally becomes clearly aware of them, seem to be those described by the Early Fathers in the first two centuries of the Church in Greece. The more you see of Athos, the more certain it seems that here, the forms of early Christianity are remembered in a way no longer true in the West.

Yet Orthodoxy, and even Athonite theology, does change, does grow, does evolve, although it does so very slowly. The strange thing is that when it does so, it seems not to change in response to individual or social pressures.

Yet there, our theology of unaided reason is regarded as a barren invention which bears no fruit, so that theory can be seen as the seedbed of heresy. If one could be certain, one might say that in this theology, the everyday forces of human society – with its unverified opinions – seem only to give rise to heresy.

Yet slow growth does occur, and again, it seemed to me then, as a relative newcomer, that the test of Tradition is the gardener's test of what to retain: *to retain the fruitful.* The theology of the *starets,* of those in whom the Spirit speaks, is seen as the True, the fruitful theology. Whether or not this view is correct, there is little doubt that on Athos the monastic idea of tradition is different in character and quality from knowledge as we define it today in the West.

The paradox *of paradocis,* then, is that the common tradition is proven not by shared demonstration, but by private experience. This is a method of verification as accurate as the scientific method, but far older. By it, Tradition proves the truth of experience, and generations of experience prove the on-going truth of Tradition.

So the *geron,* the elder, in whom the inner experience has made visible the truth of the Tradition, is the true scientist of this kind of knowledge. He it is who contains the Tradition.

Thus the 'Science' of Athos is based on evidence, but on evidence that conforms to entirely different and older rules from those of the physical sciences. Its rules provide the criteria by which we can judge our inner experience.

One of the principles of this science, it seems to me, is that the evidence it requires is often known only in the moment: unexpected; instantaneous; spontaneous. *"The wind bloweth where it listeth, and thou hearest the sound thereof, but canst not tell whence it cometh, and whither it goeth: so is every one that is born of the Spirit."* (John 3:8)

The doxology chanted by the monks puts it: *"In Thy light we shall see light."*

There is a certain practical significance to this, but it cannot always be put into writing, although it is of great importance to the Christian whose aim is to grow closer to God. The divine is not simply and directly describable, and thus there is neither demonstrable nor dialectical proof of it.

The only proof that exists is *'given proof.'* (The *'docis'* root of *'paradocis,'* the Greek word for tradition, means 'given.') This refers to proof given to individuals, and not repeatable on demand. (According to some, of course, it is *'not scientific.'*)

Today, the existence of this unscientific proof has been forgotten, for nowadays we do not trust our own experience.

FATHER I AGAIN

In another meeting with Father I, I remarked that I was beginning to see these things differently, and Father I was clearly pleased that there had been a change in me of this kind. I think that perhaps he would approve of any change, see any change as in some way God-given. I feel that this Athonite attitude is revealing: a most promising sign of the kind of understanding which exists on Athos, not just in a few rare men, but probably in a large proportion of the monks.

Before he left me that night, Father I recommended a more recent book by Father Sophrony. He lent me his copy for my brief stay in the monastery.

Afterward, we discussed, partly in relation to the book he lent me, the idea of humility, of 'making oneself nothing.' I have for a long time been aware of the paradox in which, by attempting to make oneself nothing, one is still asserting oneself.

He had a similar view. One has to attempt this, I was told, but it is not really possible without the help of God, without Christ's assistance.

CHAPTER 5

AGRYPNIA: AN ALL NIGHT VIGIL

Vigils are for remembering our spiritual life, hence their long if varying duration. This is why one of the best known of Athos' hermits during recent years was supposed to have said about an unusually long service that: *"Fifteen hours is too long. Twelve or thirteen is reasonable, but fifteen hours is just too long!"*

But I was not aware of this story when – within a minute or so of the bell – I emerged from my room at Simonos Petra, and hovered, with the evening-sunlight streaming in the window, at the top of the staircase down to the Katholikon. I was simply wondering when the vigil would begin, but had I then known this old story, I might have been less eager.

"Not yet," said the guest house master, returning to duty. *"Ten minutes, and then it rings again. Then you can go in."*

We returned to our benches. A tide of activity built up in the monastery, and then the bell again: three slow strokes, then three more slow, then seven fast: the 3-3-7 pattern, repeated several times. (I think the sequence is 1-2-3, 1-2-3, 1-2-3-4-5-6-7; then again.)

As we walked into the narthex of the Church, past the big modern frescoes beside the door, the tapping of the wooden *semantron* – an ancient Athos tradition – approached down the corridor. Monks ducked through the iron door in ones and twos, closing it gently with a solid clunk, then kissed the icons either side of the archway. Most of them went on into the next room, the *litei*. The service began softly, with single voices in the background. The church at this stage was almost entirely dark, with no more than four or five tiny flames to light it.

The sanctuary was opened, and the priests – still in their black monastic robes – could be seen dimly by the light of many candles. Between the speaking and the singing, it seemed as if they were enacting tableaux, many of them with striking similarities to some of the more common icon designs. (*"No,"* said one of the monks, *"The icons are derived from the liturgy."*)

I remembered then what I had once heard about the language of symbolism ... the language that conveys more than words, and particularly conveys more to the heart. Surely this was an example, but if so, there was no quick way of comprehending it; only repeated exposure would do it, especially from the restricted vantage point available to the 'unorthodox' that night. One thing that was noticeable was what seemed a degree of precision, of care in posture and positioning, and in getting the tableaux visually correct. What was very clear was that too much explanation, too much information, given in simplified form for tourists, would not help, but would prevent any real understanding of whatever 'message' was borne in this drama.

DARKNESS IN THE KATHOLIKON

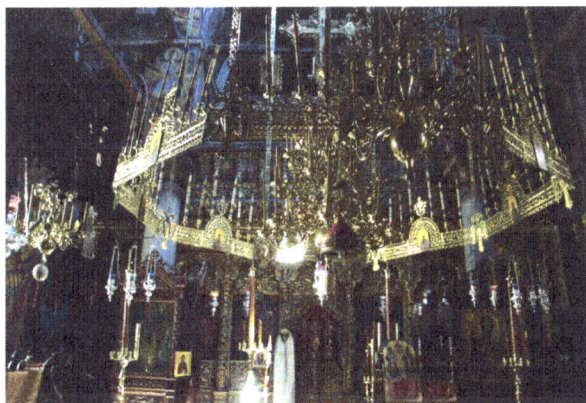

Polyeleos (RA)

As the hours passed, and the service grew more complex, I noticed that the yellow light was becoming brighter. In the domed Katholikon, a monk with a long pole was lighting the candles of the great chandelier, the *polyeleos,* one by one. Was this symbolic, perhaps, of the uncreated light arising at many points within the darkness, that darkness of the cave that occurs in so many icons, and which symbolizes the true 'poverty of spirit,' that consciousness-without-content which can by grace be found within us? This light exists within everyone, but within us, *"the darkness comprehendeth it not."* (John 1:5) It is met sometimes in prayer, or – I have heard – when we are very close to death. Meeting it changes us.

69

Next, a monk, with his smoking taper at the top of a long pole, lit the candles of a smaller central chandelier. Then he set both chandeliers swinging, the whole image a great symbol showing emergence of the light both within and without: to the stars, but also to the communicant, an 'infusion' that brings joy and health to every cell in the body.

The brass coronet of the great chandelier, some twelve feet across, twisted thirty degrees on long chains which dropped down out of the darkness of the dome. Then it checked and swung back. It continually repeated this movement, while within it, the smaller chandelier rotated in close circular orbit.

Below, the monks passed in their black robes. The chanting continued in the background. The whole pattern conjured up images of the *Mevlevi mukabele,* that strange ceremony of J'al al-Din Rumi's whirling dervishes, which celebrates the turning of the planets. They make their escape from self-concern by this strange circling ceremony.

AN IMAGE OF THEOSIS

It is difficult to clearly arrange the memories of that night in proper time sequence. I remember the arrival of the Abbot. Some time after the start of the service, two monks came in by the door near where I sat. I heard a staff tap the floor once. The new arrivals kissed the icons, then passed-on, into the nave and then into the sanctuary.

Again the staff tapped once.

In instant obedience, the pattern of activity in the church changed. The *geron* stood there, and dark figures came to him one by one, each helping to transform him, clothing him with rich vestments of gold, with a surplice covered with black crosses such as those shown on Athos on the icons of Saint Nicholas and other saints. The staff, when I saw it later, was black, with a Y-shaped head formed of two leaping golden fish, most impressive.

Now the Abbot took charge of the ceremony. In the intervals between the singing, his voice sounded loud and sonorous. The priests began to appear in rich vestments instead of monastic black. A door was opened into the sanctuary, ablaze with candles.

I did not understand much of what was going on, but was struck by the close co-ordination of the priests, unbroken at a time when monks were still coming and going to the church, as they did throughout the long ceremony. The whole service became an icon of authority without automatism: of true spiritual unity.

Now there were recognizably different stages, making the whole long vigil into an icon of *Theosis:* deification, the entry of man into God through the entry of God into man. At one stage, the priests were kissed on both cheeks by the Abbot, one by one – again reminiscent.

There was a great deal of movement between the two sanctuaries. Later I saw one of the monks lighting the candles on the smaller single chandelier in the nave of the church. The candles in the sanctuary had been extinguished, the veil drawn, and the activity and the light moved into the open church. An elaborate stand was placed in the doorway, and an icon placed on it with great reverence. Around this icon, priests circumambulated. For some time, just one priest, my friend Father I, with book and candle. Then the age ended, as it were ... the light in the nave was extinguished, the veil opened, and the great chandeliers were ablaze and swinging yet again.

It was about this time that, lulled by the chanting and the penetrating stillness of the service, I fell asleep in my seat ... leaving all as mystery.

During the night, the service went through these changing phases several times. Sometimes, there were only two candles alight in the whole center of the Katholikon. Then monks with poles lit the candles on the central chandelier, and started it swinging – side to side, rotate and stop, rotate the other way, and stop again. As it swung, during each of these prolonged periods, the candle-light reflecting off the walls moved and danced, reminding me again of Plato's famous cave analogy.

Then yet another period of darkness, and I began to drop-off to sleep again. Waking briefly, I crept off softly to bed, to be woken much later – by bell and semantron – for the continuation of the service in the very early morning. With some difficulty, I dressed and returned to my place at the rear of the Church.

There I watched, as the same pattern of the service continued, this time taking the form of a mass in which everyone, monks and lay, participated. After two or three more hours, the service ended without any visible warning, and we all trooped off to the dining hall.

Before we sat, the Abbot came in formally in procession. Everyone stood silent, as, with two monks holding the corners of his cloak, he walked to the head of the hall and sat down to eat. This time we enjoyed a special feast with enormous triangular steaks of some large but nameless fish, as well as the usual cold soup and salad. There was also a kind of crumbly dessert, all served in enameled metal bowls. At the end of this meal, there was a short service of thanks, administered in the refectory by the Abbot, then everyone dispersed for a necessary rest.

By the third time I attended one of these *agrypnia* services, I had somehow developed enough stamina to stay awake throughout the service, though during the previous two days I had walked great distances on the paths between monasteries.

The effect on me was quite remarkable. I can only assume that the duration of the effort had produced a significant change in my state of mind and body, a change I can only describe as 'firming-up' the solar plexus, perhaps the same as the development of what the Japanese call *hara*.

Strangely, this firming was both physical and psychological in its implications, the latter element being of greater significance. It served in some way as an antidote to the stress and the laxity of modern life. I cannot really explain this, but I can thoroughly recommend it to anyone who finds himself becoming soft in a soft-centered world. As a difficult and therefore effective beginning to true asceticism, I suspect it is unmatched.

We have no modern theories that are nearly large enough to contain or explain the power of the *agrypnia*. Because of this, I suspect it will never enter the life of the West in its complete form or its full power.

72

Monastery of Gregoriou, view from jetty (RA)

Often, people only stay one night in a monastery. After two days in Simonos Petra, I was expected to move on. So Father I called me aside for a moment. *"What are you going to do today?"* he asked me. *"I suggest go to Gregoriou. Then perhaps the next day you could go by boat to Panteleimon. At least you'll find it quiet.*

"Gregoriou is very good, and you could ask the 'hotelier'... the guest house master ... for a Father S. He is from Peru, but he speaks very good English. But be tactful, they are very protective of their church, and may not like the non-Orthodox in there. Some people here are afraid the unorthodox will steal their sacrament. Go and rest, and I will do the same. When you are ready to leave, ask some-one to tell me, and I will come and say goodbye."

We parted, he to his cell, and I to the guest-house once again. *"Where are you going?"* asked the guest-master in French as I reached the hall of the guest house. *"Dafni?"*

"Non," I replied, in my schoolboy version of the same language, *"je part a Gregoriou."* So the decision was made. I would move on to the next monastery down the coast. It was by then about 10:30 am, and the track to Gregoriou was supposedly a one-hour walk, most of it downhill, but I had already some experience of the time estimates given for walking on Athos. Also, I had less than the usual amount of sleep because of last night's vigil.

So I decided to rest for a while, yet leave quite early in the day. As I waited on the high balcony, guests continued to come and go, so, rather than trying to sleep, I sat on a seat alternately reading and simply watching the view below. By now, I had become less nervous about this balcony, and was even happy leaning on the railing as I enjoyed looking down onto the terraced vegetable gardens so far below, watching the few birds that had ventured out this early in the morning. I next watched some mules wandering up the zigzag path, seemingly unattended. Later, a party came up the path, from the shore or from Gregoriou: two young men in shirtsleeves, and an American priest, his heavy robes contoured with white residues of perspiration after the hot steep climb. The guest-master brought me coffee and loukoumi, again delightful.

I ate, drank, continued my restful reading for some little while longer, and pondered on what I had seen in the church. A little understanding seemed to be leaking through.

There was a pattern here that was different from things in Western Europe. Some things were more rigid, others more flexible. For example, anybody can ask a monk he trusts to become his spiritual director. Some exceptional monks are allowed to open their cells in later life, and will then be available to guide many people. It is these monks who most commonly become known as *'geron'* or *'starets.'*

So there was this flexibility. There is the much greater valuation of experience than in the Western churches. This was once expressed in the following way: *"The Eastern tradition has never made a sharp distinction between mysticism and theology; between personal experience of the divine mysteries and the dogma affirmed by the Church. Far from being opposed, theology and mysticism support and complete each other."*

This is why, on Athos, they are very firm that certain aspects of doctrine should not be changed, and also firm about the sacraments.

It was in watching the services that I began to understand why. To me, one aspect of the services appeared to be a means of transmitting attitudes, and, by doing so, helping to open people to new and more spiritual influences. If this is true, the rigidity about certain things is justified. It must be in part by its obedience to Tradition, particularly when transmitting specific spiritual attitudes, that Orthodoxy achieves its purpose of assisting people who wish to come closer to God.

I would have thought about this more, but the level of chatter and activity in the guest house continued to build up. Eventually, I decided that the best thing was to get going and find out how things were at Gregoriou. I finished packing my bag, filled my water bottle, tidied my bed, then found the guest-master and asked for Father I. At the time, I imagined the guest-master to be French, as he only spoke French to me, and, like a Parisian, refused to accept my mispronunciations – but I later learned that he is Greek.

Anyway, on this occasion we had another of our Anglo-French non-communication bouts, in which I detected the word *'cellurement'* (which was probably his term for the fact that Father I was still in his cell). I eventually gathered that Father I was not to be disturbed at this time. I wrote a brief note, placed it in the book he had lent me, and gave this book to the guest-master. *"Who is it for?"* He demanded. *"Father I,"* I told him. Thanking him for his and his monastery's hospitality, I shouldered my bag, picked up my crude staff, and left.

DOWN THE CLIFF

Soon, I wished I had waited another hour or two for Father I. I did not know which path to take. Which was the path to Gregoriou? Where did everyone go? Eventually, I decided to try the passage under the bathhouse, by the main door of the monastery, just by where the mules were stabled. I walked through the arch and found myself on the downhill zigzag-track to Simonos Petra's little harbor, which seemed to lie almost vertically below.

My map showed this as joining the path to Gregoriou high up, almost directly below Simonos Petra monastery. However, from the guest house balcony, I could see a path round the next headland, low-down so that it seemed near to the sea.

So I continued down the path, looking for a junction. The first gate I found had a ladder leaning on it. I decided dubiously this was unlikely to be frequently-opened, and walked on. Many times the path divided. After a while, I learned to recognize which was the main path, and which section, often no wider than the path, was not a path at all, but one of many narrow terraced olive-groves that lie alongside the path down most of its fall to the sea. I went on down: one hundred feet, I estimated, two hundred, three hundred. Still no division. Still nothing to tell me I was on the right path. An iron pipe followed the path, with water-taps for thirsty climbers.

From there, when I left, it was a long steep climb, down the stone track between the fields and trees, to a quayside more than seven hundred feet below, then along the shore, up and down over successive headlands; and so I wound down, above the shoreline, to some rather beautiful small buildings with a roof over a small seat – presumably a shelter for those who walked between monasteries. I stopped to rest and pray a moment, then continued. Always the path was the same, a mule track with diagonal ridges of worn limestone across the path every four or five feet. Again, I saw the occasional sheet metal mule-shoe. The trees and the terracing seemed in good repair.

I had been thinking for some time that I had lost the path, so that I should have to go all the way down to the jetty and await the afternoon boat, when I finally found the junction more than half-way down, at one of the bends in the track. The mule track there did not turn until it reached the edge of a ravine that lay between this part of the mountain and the headland hiding Gregoriou. The direction was marked by a small whitewashed shrine with dome, windows, cross, another concrete seat shaded by a roof, and, on the pillars supporting the roof, the sign: 'M.GRIGORIOU,' on a blue plate, with an arrow pointing into the bushes at the side of the path, right on the edge of the ravine ...

I rested there again a few minutes, hitched my bag a little higher, and turned to the side path. This was the worst track I came across on Athos, (of the few I had seen by then.) In many places, it was only eighteen inches wide, clinging to the side of the ravine. The first few 'legs' were of smoothed stones, many just lying where they had been found, others apparently arranged at random.

Often they were sloping away, so that a slip would take one off the path, if one simply put too much weight in the wrong place. Then there were sections where the path was no more than foot-wide grooves cut in the earth, normally with bushes and some rocks between them and the steep slope. All of it demanded some agility.

This path continued down some four-hundred-feet to sea-level, ending in a beautiful rock-walled cove. Inland were the most enormous boulders, worn smooth by winter torrents, although the ravine was now summer-dry. Between them grew a tangle of trees – figs, a fallen sweet chestnut surrounded by smaller chestnuts, something like laurel, but with red papery bark. Nothing moved but the waves, softly washing the beach.

A mark confirmed the path, up from the cove into the next headland, passing at some distance from a house I had seen from above, a red-tiled house amid the trees of the ravine. After a swig of water and a few minutes sitting on a boulder, I set off again. I walked alongside a barbed-wire fence opposite a wild fig, past a locked gate, beside a shaded concrete seat for travelers, with a painted cross on the white-washed wall behind the seat.

The path here was wider, obviously designed for mule-traffic, well-maintained, although the house in the ravine, with its white walls and large vine covered loggia, seemed entirely without movement. Here the stones of the path were better set. There was enough width everywhere. It was here, too, that I first saw the big cacti that are common on that part of Athos, and here, too, I met a party coming from Gregoriou: four young Germans. I recognized them as having been on the same boat with me from Ouranoupolis. I greeted them, and as most of them spoke good English, we were able to exchange information. Gregoriou was not very far, they told me, and asked what the path to Simonos Petra was like. They knew about the climb.

I let them pass, and then continued on my way, now uphill a little to rise above the cliffs at the end of the headland. In the distance, I heard an amplified woman's voice speaking German. It was a tour-boat passing-by. After a few minutes the voice shifted to a different language. I think the same commentary, repeated very loud. In 1045 AD, the Byzantine emperor, Constantine Monomachos, had prohibited women on Athos. One result of this edict is a growing number of tour boats, from which large numbers of visitors strive to see the place they are not allowed to enter. Today, no boat with women aboard is allowed within five hundred meters of the peninsula.

With the distant commentary as background, I continued up the gentle, stony slope to the end of the headland, turned the corner, and there again was the peak of Mount Athos, and below it, the bulk of a monastery tucked-in against the cliffs at one end of a small track. The track widened, and in time became a stone-paved road, branching up again into the woods above.

The signs of careful maintenance were ever more apparent. In one place a circular 'tower' wall some eight-feet high supported a single olive tree. In another, stones sticking out from an eight-foot high wall provided simple steps, giving access to an olive-grove immediately above the road ... Then I followed a gradual curve, down to the bottom of the cove with its inevitable dried-out, boulder-lined stream. In this case, it was crossed by a workmanlike, Land Rover-width, concrete bridge marked with a circle of red paint, the sign that – in many places in Athos – indicates a main pathway between monasteries.

I was heading in the right direction.

CHAPTER 6

PROSEVCHI: DIRECTED PRAYER

Fresco (G)

"Lord Jesus Christ, Son of God, have mercy on me, a sinner."

On my first visit to Simonos Petra, I had mentioned to Father I my interest in the Jesus prayer, that repetitive-prayer that was based on the invocation of the name of Jesus, which seems to form the basis of many individual practices on the Mountain. We discussed this in more depth. In our discussions, I used the word 'method.' I said that I had in the past tried to use the Jesus prayer as a method. My memory of his words is imperfect, but I shall try to recapture as much of the sense as possible. *"It is not quite that,"* he told me, *"the Jesus Prayer is not a method. Properly, it is a relationship, something personal, emotional.*

"If one treats it as a method, intellectually, then you are missing the whole point, the main point of it, which is a slowly developing relationship with the person of Jesus.

"It is just like speaking to someone in the ordinary way. Only then will it grow, will it change, will it lead to something new. Then, everything else will grow from that relationship."

Like many true things, this approach, in which things 'grow' at their own pace, doesn't entirely 'make sense' to Western reason, which views the significance of human life – in any situation we meet – as a matter of 'doing something.' But on Athos, I was having to learn not to rely on our ordinary kind of reason, for it is a poor guide in this strange country of the spirit. The whole idea of a 'method' seems to belong to what modern thought calls the 'left-brain.' In modern Western man, the 'dominant hemisphere' or 'doing brain' is regarded as that part of the mind that governs voluntary actions, and whose thinking is shaped accordingly. However, I thought, even then, that this division might act differently in different civilizations, for instance, in the Japanese.

Certainly, this part of the mind, as shaped today by our rationalist culture, is in some strange way incompetent in the world of prayer. Prayer as it progresses depends more on a relinquishing of control than on intensified control, although I have discovered that – at least on Athos – silent prayer actually demands attentiveness and even purpose. *'Prosevchi:'* directed or attentive prayer, the word often used in the passages of the *Philokalia* which talk about prayer, involves a certain directing-of-attention.

But this is difficult to understand, because it is not an active control, but instead, involves what one can only call *'effortless effort.'* This is not really surprising, as the Jesus prayer is essentially *'hesychastic'* in its nature, and *hesychia*, the deep stillness of the heart, is entirely incompatible with our active, Western idea of intellectually controlled action. Over-activity destroys, or to use one modern psychological term, 'masks' such states from our attention.

Non-doing

Paradoxically, this question – that of 'controlling without doing' – is linked with another big question, that of how to bring suitable emotions to the point of prayer. A 'doing' attitude, an 'atomist' or anthropocentric attitude that *'I am doing it; I am praying,'* actually prevents this. It has been suggested that it does so by causing inappropriate activity. Unlike this, employing the correct *'hesychastic energies,'* to coin a term for a concept that is lacking from the English dictionary, makes us sensitive to the personal and the emotional. These energies make us want to pray, and only when we want to pray can we give *attention* to our prayer throughout the time of prayer, thus fulfilling one meaning of the Biblical idea that we should *"pray without ceasing."* (Thessalonians 5:17)

Yet these energies, unlike the active energies of modern life, convey stillness, and this paradoxical link between the stillness and activity is an essential ingredient of prayer.

This comes always with a sense of something greater than ourselves; of dependence on God, and on His Holy Spirit.

Attention

In simpler terms, one common result of our Western idea that we can 'do' everything is that normally we confuse control and attention. These are often seen as one and the same, but in fact, they are only linked by the fact that attention is needful before we can control anything.

The distinction between care and doing is associated with the difference between the different roles of our two hands, especially during activities like writing or drawing. For a normal right-handed person, the right hand carries out the action while the left hand fulfills a less active but equally essential role, positioning the object on which the right hand works.

In prayer, the two are no longer mutually active. In prayer we must minimize movement but at the same-time intensify attention. The word, *prosevchi,* attentive prayer, links with another Greek word, *prosochi,* used for care and attentiveness in general.

Prosochi and *prosevchi* are undoubtedly 'left hand' activities. One experiences the necessity for this kind of care in any person-to-person communication.

If one person takes too firm a 'right-hand' control of a conversation, the other person normally feels shut out of proper communication. Communication requires a certain attentive flexibility, and this only comes when one recognizes somebody to be a person. It requires a degree of humility. It requires 'left handed' attentiveness.

This is especially true of prayer. This same personal aspect, Father I told me, was the whole essence of Christianity as the monk of Athos sees it. Earlier religions, before Christianity, seem to have viewed their God as too far, too immaterial, too impersonal. Then there was Jesus, and one might learn to relate to Jesus as person (Gr. *prosopos*). Then, if one's mind could reach this far, one could get help.

It works in practice; this personal relationship, this kind of relaxation, begins to bring the right energies to prayer. I have had this demonstrated many times. But then we forget, and have to experiment again inside ourselves to re-establish the personal element. This special idea of the 'personal' is not only found in Athonite theology. It is described in Martin Buber's well-known book: '*I and Thou.*' One can have an '*I-it*' relationship, mechanical, or as modern thought would put it, syntactical. Or one can have an '*I-thou*' relationship, a heart relationship ... with an emotional content. True prayer involves heart relationships.

Have you ever seen a 'master-class' in which the master of some art teaches the pupils by leading their *attention* into ignored corners of their skill, illumining all the usually ignored details of the actions needed? Whatever the 'craft,' this is a master's way of teaching. I first glimpsed this skill on a later visit to Athos, when I witnessed an impromptu master-class given to the monks of Gregoriou by the giant Master-chanter of Athos, Dionysius Firfiris; the power and precision of his traditional Greek chanting was only equaled by the breadth of his sense-of-humor.

The late 19th century version of the Jewish mystical tradition put it in a different way: it said that we must find *'Microprosopus:'* the 'small countenance,' before we can know *'Macroprosopus:'* the 'great countenance.'

JESUS PRAYER

The Greek version of the Jesus prayer is, in full: *"Kyrie Iesou Christe, Yie tou Theou, Eleison me ton amartalon."* In English, it is: *"Lord Jesus Christ, Son of God, have mercy on me, a sinner."*

There are different versions, and also different ways of praying, but the Jesus prayer expresses two principles: one is that short prayer is the most direct and simplest way to heaven. The other relates to the third section, *'Eleison me,' 'Lord have mercy on me.'*

"This," I was told, *"is asking for something you have already received. It should be thankful, not heavy and self* disparaging."

More than that, if it is said persistently and carefully, in the simplest prescribed form, it will have an on-going cumulative effect, energizing the interior life of our psyche. A small detail, yet its results in practice can be considerable, as I have already discovered. But we must also remember our need for mercy. If we can give enough time to this process, it can lead upwards, in progressive steps to complete transformation.

Prayer depends upon our humility. What I was first told about the Jesus Prayer was clearly echoed by Father S, a monk I met later in the monastery of Gregoriou. It was prayer, and especially the Jesus prayer, that was the key. If one was praying in the heart, then everything would be alright. The monks also say the same for the liturgy; when it is performed as originally created, it puts things right. When these things were right, it was implied, there was less need to think about one's life and one's work, and about anything one should do, (which was the way in which I had been praying up until that time).

If one prayed and developed the personal links to Jesus, all would change in ways we could not predict, and all would be well. He made no attempt to talk me into joining the Orthodox Church.

(*"When the apple is ripe,"* Said Father S about this on another occasion, *"it will fall!"*)

The sacraments were important, but, equally as important, it was the prayer. I just had to pray. Probably that would bring me to the Orthodox Church, but if not, that too would be God's will; if the prayer went right, whatever happened would be right.

THE SEMANTRON AND THE ARK

Semantron used to call monks to prayer (Jovanvb)

Without prayer, even one's humility is false. But the intention is important, it is necessary to try for true humility even before being helped in prayer. During the night, with only the fitful light of cheap hurricane lamps, I had gone to sleep around 8:30. Before four, the bells rang for the early morning service, and I had my first introduction to that instrument of Athonite discipline, the *'semantron.'*

This is a shaped plank of wood. It is beaten with a mallet, and some say that it is meant to sound like a thousand monks hurrying to church at once, all with wooden shoes. At least, that is what it does sound like!

The semantron was invented during the Turkish occupation of Greece, a 'night' that lasted more than four-hundred years. When the ringing of bells had been prohibited by the conquerors, other ways had to be found of calling the worshipers to services.

It is also worth recording the symbolic interpretation. This hammering is said to represent the noise made by Noah when building the ark.

Normally, there are three repetitions of this rhythm before a service, and a mnemonic says of these repetitions that: *"one is to call the birds, one the beasts, and one to call men."*

SURRENDER INTO THE HANDS OF GOD

On a later visit, I met a problem which was typical of the whole difficulty of getting to Athos. Because of some hiatus in the circumstances, I needed to go back into Athos, and then leave Athos again by Thursday, while the offices from which I had to obtain the documents needed to get into Athos would not open again to the public until 11 am on Monday, and those offices were in bustling Thessaloníki, still 140 km from the Ouranoupolis pier where the Athos ferry sailed at 9:45 every morning.

Here was the real test of nearly thirty years of prayer. In spite of the uncertainties, it seemed important that I go. So we decided just that: to go anyway. If it was right that I should go to Athos, then something would resolve the difficulties, though I could not imagine what. Just what happened in this particular instance will be revealed later in the book. For now, it is more important to consider the general principle underlying this essential but often forgotten dimension of Christianity

We must leave ourselves in the hands of God, and by this, must test our intention, stated immediately after my previous visit, to place my wellbeing in God's hands. This is important to understand: it is oneself, one's intentions, one's emotional condition, one's constancy, which such situations test. They do not 'test for truth,' or discover for us whether God is real; they test us and our ability to live with the reality of a living God. Such a test is a question of our attitude.

If we are unwilling to see it as a test of ourselves, then it becomes a challenge to God and, as the Gospel puts it; *"thou shalt not test the Lord thy God."* (The word 'tempt' – in our English version – actually translates the Greek *'peirasmos:'* the temptation which tries and tests us.)

True tests of our faith – or the lack of it – exist in all situations of uncertainty, and sometimes depend, not so much on ourselves and our everyday methods of making sure, as, like St. Paul as he sailed these coasts in much more difficult days, on doing what we can, even when we are unsure, and then leaving the rest to God and His *'synergia'* to send what He will.

It was this, it seemed: a true change of intent, a reversal in the direction of our will, which must demonstrate a genuine change of heart.

I suspect also that this is not something that happens without effort, but something which happens only as long as we have in mind *Mneme Theou:* which means remembrance of God. We have to remember God: *'Mneme Theou,'* but normally we forget the Greek word *'alithea.'* (Remember the river of forgetfulness, *'Lethe,'* in Greek mythology). *"Remembering gives us its opposite:* "*'alithea,' truth."* (To quote Abbot George of the monastery of Gregoriou.)

About that time, two Englishmen, a clergyman and a social worker, visited the Athos monastery of Simonas Petra while I was there. After seeing the demanding regime, they began to ask some very familiar questions, questions which are now being asked by so-called theologians in Greece. *'Why bother?'* they asked, again and again. *'How does all this help our fellow man?'* They demanded to know: *'Why are you not more concerned with all the sickness and injustice in the world?'*

"They did not understand us," a novice told me in quiet simplicity. For these are old questions, although understandable. In medieval times, they were traditionally answered by using the Gospel story of Martha and Mary. Martha is the well-known symbol of Christian labor in the world, Mary of the work of the monk and the mystic, whose work is essential for mankind, yet is necessarily different from the jobs that most people perform in the world.

For many people, this difference is difficult to understand. This is yet another reason why Mount Athos is known as *Panagia's* Garden: because it is here that Mary's work is done, not that of Martha. But what is the work of Mary: what is the point of all the effort made by the monks? It is the great work of remembering God: *Mneme Theou.*

This *Mneme Theou* is an essential element in a life of *metanoia,* a precisely defined form of repentance.

Icon of Mary from Gregoriou Monastery (RA)

CHAPTER 7

SEVENTH VISIT – ATHONITE FAITH

All this relates to the fact that the true Athos experience of faith, the true Christian experience, is not a merely intellectual change in belief. This is a true *'change of heart,'* as described in our quotation from Isaiah a few paragraphs below. It begins with *metanoia,* seen as a change in the purpose from which one's life is motivated, a change which shifts the center of one's being from one's small-self to God Himself.

NEED FOR PRAYER

"We need prayer and worship to help us to remember God. The world is too strong, it takes us away, distracts us, makes us forget," said Abbot George once. *"The nations today live an anthropocentric life, a life of lithea, everyone centered on themselves. We need a 'Theocentric' life, a life of 'alithea'"* (a word for 'truth' in the New Testament). *"Living in the world causes the human personality to become fragmented. These anthropocentric or man-centred ideas, attitudes and actions are 'hamartia:' sin. They divide us internally, and they also divide us one from another."*

The point, then, is not that there is no need to care for people in the world, but that the work of Martha depends on the secret labors of Mary: to draw a very simplistic analogy, psychologically speaking, it is Martha that has the car, Mary the fuel. Only spiritual strength can resolve the causes of the problems whose symptoms are so ably and necessarily identified by the social worker. The priest and the social worker should always serve together, but they should not serve, as they so often do today, in identical ways. The work of the social worker is that of Martha, that of the monk – and often of the priest – is that of Mary. Both are needed. The world needs Martha, but Martha needs Mary. The two together express the ancient theological idea of *'synergia.'* The Athos experience slowly makes it clear that, without remembering, nothing remains true, for when we forget ourselves, everything begins to decline.

As soon as we remember, everything grows true again. Then Christ appears in us ... then, progressively, we get the right energies, the right 'spirit,' the right strengths in the right places. The 'center of gravity' of anthropocentric, self-centered man is biased towards one part of himself or another. The 'center of gravity' of the Theocentric man is in the heart, and is universal and unifying. It is then, when we are centered in the heart, that the *image and likeness of God within us* (Genesis 1:26) comes to life.

This is the beginning of 'holiness,' or spiritual wholeness, not self-centered, but God-centered. Unity within-us exists only in combination with an external unity, the birth of Christ within us with participation in the 'mystical body' without. Inside and outside are never really divided.

The *'Theocentric man,'* he who emerges in this union of inner and outer, is described in Isaiah 11, one of the classical prophecies of the birth of Christ. *"And there shall come forth a rod out of the stem of Jesse, and a branch shall grow out of his roots: And the spirit of the Lord shall rest upon him, the spirit of wisdom and understanding, the spirit of counsel and might, the spirit of knowledge and of the fear of the Lord; And shall make him of quick understanding in the fear of the Lord: and he shall not judge after the sight of his eyes, neither reprove after the hearing of his ears; but with righteousness shall he judge the poor, and reprove with equity for the meek of the earth."* (Isaiah 11: 1-4)

But if this is difficult to remember for a moment, it is more difficult still to remember continually. Our head cannot do this; only the heart can do it.

This solution depends on our learning practical methods unfamiliar to Western man. One such practical solution to the question of remembering was given, again by Abbot George of Gregoriou, when he said about the difficulty of remembering that:

"Mneme Theou goes together with 'mneme thanatos:' remembrance of death with a realization of our mortality. They belong together. Mneme thanatos leads to real mneme Theou."

"Jesus said: 'Let him who seeks, not cease seeking until he finds, and when he finds, he will be troubled, and when he has been troubled, he will marvel, and he will reign over the All.'" (Gospel according to Thomas)

Whether or not it is true that Athos is the heart of Christendom, this 'last autonomous monastic republic in the world,' as it has been called, is certainly the home of a Christianity *of the heart.*

Athonite religion is different from much modern religious thought, which sees religion as a question of attitude and ethics that must be reached rationally. In this personally-unsatisfying, theoretical type of Western religion, there is little difference between religion and personal opinion. It seems now clear to me that true Christianity, matured in the Athonite model, is entirely different from this in its basic form; that it depends not on the relation between ideas and our often unsuccessful attempt to obey our own ideas, but on emotions, emotional attitudes, and on the relation of these to experience. This view demands and develops an altogether wider range of experience than that considered by modern philosophy. Ideas and dogmas exist in this, but play a very secondary role in it all.

Paradoxically, Athos does serve as a source of new ideas in one area where we in the West are short of clear conceptualizations: in the area of emotion itself. The English-speaking peoples at least have today a very limited and self indulgent view of emotion. Athos may well serve to provide us with wholly new ideas about emotion, and indeed it is these new ideas about emotion which form almost the whole subject matter of this book. So important is this that I will begin, right here, by summarizing some of the most important of the ideas you are likely to meet in these pages.

With the change of heart, essential to the Christianity that exists on Athos, comes a change in our experiencing. I will try to provide some kind of example of this, taken from one of my earlier visits to the mountain.

CEMETERY CHAPEL

Cemetery Chapel (RA)

What I am about to describe happened when the long Matins service was at an end, after nearly four hours of prayer and chanting. Visible through the carvings of the *iconostasis,* the many reflections of candles on brass still formed the strongest image in the great monastery church. It was then, on my sixth visit to Athos, that my friend, the priest Father A came up to me in the carved, semi-circular row of choir stalls of the great monastery church and invited me to join him. Leaving the older monks to their prayers, we walked down the length of the church and went out of the narthex, up the steps under the fig tree to a small gate at the rear of the monastery. There, he produced a great key from beneath his robes and, unlocking the gate, we exited through. Once out, we passed down a short path to the domed cemetery chapel, where it overlooked the sea. Inside, the Father found time in his demanding schedule to show me the frescoes.

Some of the paintings in that chapel are truly magnificent. It would not be proper or adequate for me to describe them in words, but they are expressive and filled with meaning. Among them, painted more than a century ago, is an impressive 'Trinity' with three faces and six arms.

But more significant for me in that state of heightened awareness that came from the service, after Father A had shown me the frescoes and the icons there, he took me outside to the little graveyard with its several wooden crosses and one larger iron cross bearing a name.

Coming straight from the great stillness of the monastery church, the graveyard somehow exuded an electrifying sense of peace and joy. My Western mind was and still is unable fully to cope with this kind of noumenal experience that seems to be so familiar to some members of the Orthodox Church. It seemed more than imaginary, yet less than objective ... and indeed this, the existence of experience that does not make intellectual 'sense,' yet which is clear and powerful enough not to be doubted or argued, is the basic paradox that meets those who penetrate beyond the ordinary 'tourist face' of Mount Athos.

FORGIVE YOUR BROTHER

As we left the cemetery chapel, Father A took me to one of the tiny chapels in the main block of the monastery. When we entered the chapel, I saw around me several familiar faces ... almost the same small group of monks as those who had invited me to join them in a liturgy to St. Christopher in the small chapel of the gardener's cottage set in the back of the monastery. I was aware of a great sense of love, of belonging, expressed by the Greek word *koinonia,* a *sense* that I have never experienced to the same degree in England, even amongst those with whom I have worked, studied, or served for years.

The celebrant, Father M, had also officiated at that earlier service. The old Father S, another friend, sat quietly at the back of the chapel, his head bowed much of the time in prayer. In the gloom, the few small candles shone on the icons and the simple furnishings.

The service began and ended in stillness.

Early in the liturgy, this sense of love and mystery overcame me, drove out my thoughts of self, and cleansing tears followed, what the early fathers called *'fire and tears.'* I began then to understand the theological significance of *koinonia*. In modern Greek theology, it is said to represent the love that unites the Trinity and whose expression between members of the church expresses the loving nature of the Trinity in a true, emotional union within the church; a kingdom of love on earth.

Now, it became real for me. It was hard to believe that, only days before, I had been playing my accustomed role in business meetings at which the whole way of life on Athos would have been regarded as nonsense. It may not make 'sense,' perhaps, but it produced the intended result. After the service, I had a great sense of what I can only call 'cleanness,' of simplicity, and of sensitivity to things of which I am in my everyday life normally unaware. More even than on my previous visits I began to understand what was really possible for a human being, and began, just began, to rediscover the incentive to make that inner effort for myself. From the midst of those causeless tears, in this strange moment, I had become emptied of myself for a while ... something very necessary for me. This, more clearly than ever before, and after six visits to the Holy Mountain, was exactly what I had been looking for.

This, the strange and practical significance of *koinonia*, explains why, in the Gospels, and often reiterated by the fathers, is this need to be reconciled to one's brother, and why the whole idea of preceding communion with reconciliation is so important to Orthodox thought even today. This idea is not only ethically valid, but in this quite different way, it is important to real religious growth. The strength to pray comes from liturgy and love. The strength of the liturgical communion, as was later clearly demonstrated to me on Mount Athos, depends on our unity with all those communicating.

An environment of love is an environment of prayer.

EMOTIONAL STILLNESS

I had begun to be hopeful on Athos when I first rediscovered for myself the strange fact, little understood in the West today, that only through this discovery, of *koinonia,* might I understand the stillness of the monk and truly religious man: that joyful-stillness that goes beyond mere 'peace of mind' – which is why it defies our rational analysis.

It was only in the memory of this 'inner resource' of Christian joy that I first began to understand the monks of Athos.

Only by keeping this in mind, could I even imagine how they face a world with so few modern comforts or distractions, a world that seems to offer them few pleasures with their many hardships. Only in the absence of *koinonia* had I begun at last to understand the failures of the more-intellectual forms of seeking I had known before. Only in its absence can we perhaps hope to understand the paradoxical-angers, the bitterness, of so many religious people.

It is this that I call *'the emotional question.'*

Not only is this implicit in the strange paradox so powerfully expressed in Eastern Christianity, with its greater intensity of both joy and suffering. It is implicit in the words and writings of the monks, particularly in the 'message' given to the Russian St. Silouan, towards the end of the last century – the message, alluded to earlier, that he should: *"keep thy soul in hell, and despair not."*

This strange saying had seemed to me, for many years, to contain some solution to our modern emotional problems, although it had often seemed to me more repellent than significant. Yet beneath its threatening exterior, I sensed something different, a direct expression of the Christian-paradox.

It was this, too, that took me to Athos.

FEAR OF GOD

Essentially, what took me to Athos was the question of how to become truly Christian, truly God-fearing, in heart as well as head.

This was the question to which Athos showed me the beginnings of an answer, an answer which the monks – those of them who have become my friends – are still helping me to work out in my life: my chance to change.

To talk or write about this is difficult. One has to touch on things difficult to experience, and even more difficult to remember. One has to talk objectively about things that are intensely personal, yet speak in terms that will link to the experiences of others. One has, in a word, to make them *'recognizable,'* at least for those who remember similar experiences. This is only possible by evoking memories long-buried in the heart, for to Athonite thinking, the heart is the home of knowledge and even of 'imaginations,' as well as of emotion.

But emotion there is: indeed, I had to rediscover what was once I believe described as 'voluntary suffering:' to undertake a strange inner asceticism of awakening painful-memories, then learning to live with them while remembering not to despair.

So I discovered, one can go beyond the despair. On Athos, this is not quite as difficult as it sounds. As a spiritual reality, the Holy Mountain is an intensification of the inner-life that lies hidden in everyone – for it is a parable and symbol of something meaningful to us all. For an English speaker, this symbolism began with a *'parable of language.'* It is not just that the letters of Greek are different. Greek as a language, and particularly the rich vowel structure of the liturgical Greek used in the monasteries, is more expressive of emotion than is English. It is as if the vowels are truly *'the emotional parts of words.'*

In this book, then, I have tried to use words whose meaning has been partially forgotten by the West. Here they serve as parables for insights whose emotional significance has also been forgotten. This means that the only way to rediscover this significance, and so to restore the meanings of these words, lies in experience. Hence the need for what I have pretentiously called *'field theology.'*

The beauties of *Panagia's* Garden are many of them hidden from the casual visitor. Some of these beauties, some of these virtues, can be understood only by those who can *'drink the medicine.'*

95

CHAPTER 8

PROLEPSIS OR PREDISPOSITION

On my second visit to Athos, I made much greater contact with the monks on the Holy Mountain. It was then, at their invitation, and with their help, that I began to penetrate past the physical and mental problems I faced simply as a result of the unfamiliar circumstances, and into the true inner life of the monasteries, particularly of the monastery of Gregoriou, where I first found – or was found by – real friends amongst the monks.

It was there, reading an English translation of the *Philokalia*, which they kept in the monastery guest house, that I began to discover something of the character of Athos. The West, after all, obtained the *Philokalia* from Athos; the work of translation was initially proposed by a hermit on Athos, the Russian Father Nikon, once a chamberlain in the Czar's court.

For Athos, the sayings of the Early Fathers that are preserved in the *Philokalia* are a prime source of understanding about their vocation, and the psychology of the *Philokalia* could be regarded as the psychology of Orthodox Greece. On Athos, then, I discovered a great difference between my memories and those of the monk. There on the Holy Mountain are men who remember 'answers' forgotten by the West: men who, even today, experience what religion once was ... what it was before we began to demand that it must all be explained ... before we began to imagine that it might be something 'purely personal,' and so different for every man and woman. On Athos there are men who seem to remember what religion was, not only before it was something generally doubted, but even before it was something to be believed-blindly.

On Athos, only faith has eyes, and doubt is blind. Faith affirms, while doubt seeks explanations. For Athos today is a living part of that earlier, Byzantine world, in which, for all its faults, religion was something not analyzed by reason, but lived by the heart.

Different people notice different things. This depends on our predispositions – *prolepses* – and at the same time it contributes to it.

Our *prolepses* depend on what we remember ... both on what memories we have 'in store,' and which of those memories are drawn out of us, and actually remembered. Any school-teacher knows that *attention decides what goes into memory*. Any psychoanalyst knows that *attention decides what comes out of memory.*

THE MONK REMEMBERS

What then is it that the monk remembers, which we no longer know? What does the hermit remember, that we so often forget? In the West it has been discovered by research – the 'tool' of the Western mind – that more than fifty per cent of people remember experiences of kinds generally 'forgotten' or ignored or devalued by our culture. The inner experiences found on Athos occur at some time for many men and women, but can sometimes be discovered there as if they are becoming commonplace and 'in the flesh.'

The particular *prolepsis*, the predisposition that makes something important to somebody, so that they rarely completely forget it – that is not so common. We live in a world that has forgotten what Christianity once was.

But here perhaps is part of the answer. It is explained in the words of one of the Athos Abbots, Father Mitrophan, of the Monastery of Hilandar, in a translation of an article written on his return from a visit to Russia. This passage shows, in its content and its character, what you might call a typical Athonite view of the world, and so in part expresses an *'Athonite prolepsis.'*

He wrote: *"It (Athos) is an offering of the world to God. Bowel and flesh and bone, from the bowels and flesh of the world. The world in every age, just as the bee fills the honeycomb with honey, fills the cells of the monasteries and the cavities of the earth with monks.*

"It is not possible for it ever to become an object of our curiosity, or even of our spiritual needs, and how much more so of our material needs. It will always remain like the priceless myrrh, poured-out profusely over the feet of Jesus.

"Inside that dark cloud, what is celebrated day after day? What else but a ceaseless, permanent reaching out to God.

"That fire, which Christ came and lit in the world, that very flame, now and always, consoles hearts whose holy destiny makes them go out of the world, once and for all, and to follow uncondi- tionally the traces of the incarnate Word, to create a tiny flock, a dynamic lever, a raising up and a support and a hope for the world ... even an invasion and a violent seizure of the Kingdom of Heaven. A new creation and state of being ... whose nourishment is the Spirit, which descends upon and is poured out in the hearts of those who seek Him.

"He sends His angels to His servants ... how much more easily will He bring you into relations with those who have the rank of His apostles – His monks.

"And if one is acquainted with a master, like him also ... he enters or rather is taken up into the sphere of his prayer. His very bones become refined and full of life. In the light he beholds light. The hand of the work which bears him is powerful, since he has com- bated with Satan in the desert, and has held onto God, like Jacob before the dawn. He has drunk the bitterness of the inferno, and has not despaired, he has drunk the life-giving water of Paradise, and has not become proud. He goes in and comes out of the gates of life freely."

But even to know such a man – this alone is not enough. It is indeed almost meaningless to those whose experience and *prolepsis* is shaped on the city streets of Western Europe or America, or even on the streets of Athens. It will make no sense to those whose view of a wider world is glimpsed from a charter-plane, hire-car, or tour- bus.

LIMITED ACCEPTANCE

The concept of *prolepsis* connects with a strange phenomenon to which, for my own convenience, I have given the somewhat colorful name of *'the law of limited acceptance.'* This does at least describe what it is about.

As I am beginning to understand this law, it involves two factors.

1. The first is that we can do little for ourselves without the action of grace.

2. The second is that, to preserve the freewill given to man by God, it seems as if this grace is received by us only to the degree to which we wish to receive it. For most people this wishing does not consist of a single general wish, but of many small choices that we must make in face of many different situations.

It is relative to this that the Old Testament truth of a 'jealous' God has its value, for the truth seems to be that His grace is not available as long as we prejudge, as long as we set specific requirements or demands upon our situation, which is for as long as we are *'half-hearted'* – which is our commonplace state. Our understanding of the active side of the mind now begins to suggest that 'half-hearted' should more properly be described as 'wrong-hearted.' The biblical analogy of hearts-of-stone springs to mind. The demands we make upon life depend on our predispositions, our *'prolepses.'* To change them, to allow them to be changed, we must no longer cling to those predispositions.

To make this clear I shall have to try to take you with me once again on another visit to the Holy Mountain itself, a visit at once imaginary, because rebuilt in my imagination, and real, because compounded, though in changed-sequence, of many experiences and conversations recalled from a whole series of visits, visits that have gone on 'behind the scenes' in the monasteries and *kellia*, and into the world of stillness normally known only to the monk.

For this, I shall have to make available to you part of my memory and, perhaps, if I am able, even a part of my *prolepsis.*

I myself only began really to understand the reality that has come to flower on Athos on my second visit, when the strains of being thrust into an unfamiliar world 'came to a head' for me. It was then, I suppose, that I first 'passed-through' what St. Gregory of Nyssa called the *'Red Sea'* in his *'Life of Moses'* – the escape from my everyday 'Egypt' of concern with business.

In terms of St. Gregory's analogy, the first stage of 'passing through' involved meeting a profound sensation of emptiness, for which he uses the analogy of the 'bitter waters;' but which later emerged into what I have since learned to regard as a kind of third stage of pilgrimage, where real communication with the monks became possible.

This happened perhaps because, by chance or by grace, I was now free to spend more time in one monastery instead of having to move on, as on previous visits. It was in these conditions that I was able slowly to 'pass through' right into that different world of Byzantium-preserved. I had time to attend all the day's services. Time for prayer. Time to learn from the monks their own way of viewing their life.

What made all this possible now was that on this occasion I had received a formal written invitation to visit the monastery of Gregoriou for 'two or three weeks' at Easter. Suddenly, those ancient iron-studded doors were open. The invitation was initially delivered verbally over lunch one Saturday in the house of Gerald Palmer, when Father S, the hieromonk I had met at Gregoriou on my first visit, was staying for a few days in England. He was sorting out publication of a small book he had written. My wife and I were invited to the house to meet him, and almost immediately we arrived, he gave me this invitation, together with some details on how to arrange to stay for longer than the four-days that are permitted for an uninvited '*Xenos.*'

As a result, I of course wrote to him when settling arrangements, and received a typed letter from the monastery that made the formalities in Greece very easy. Finally, the day came: a fine sunny morning on Easter Saturday. (That year, the Greek Easter was five weeks later than its Western date).

I gave up my passport on the quay as before, and took the eight-forty-five boat to Dafni, followed down the coast of Athos by a school of dolphins sporting in the waves of the boat's wash, a living Easter omen, and the first time I had seen dolphins since my childhood.

LORRY TO KARYES

Pilgrim ferry arriving (RA)

This time, when the boat arrived at Dafni, the now familiar bus was not there. Instead, in the peak of the Easter rush of pilgrims, two-lorries, one very small, waited by the quayside. Greece has not yet entered into the 'information civilization'. By the time I had discovered, (not speaking Greek,) that these lorries were there for us because there was no bus, they were almost full, and I just managed to squeeze aboard, standing precariously against a side less than two-feet high.

About that ride I shall say little: my position was insecure, the road precipitous, and often was of nothing but sand, which created great dust clouds. I was grateful to arrive at last, somewhat stiff and sore, but at least whole and in one piece, in Karyes. It is in things like this that the real frictions of such a journey often exist. In the West today, we make a fetish not only of being safe, but of feeling safe. One trip up the road to Karyes in that overloaded lorry, and one begins to learn not to be so concerned with feeling safe. In fact, I have found that this effect is cumulative. The once-terrifying bus that ordinarily takes that route today now seems nothing to worry about.

The once-terrifying balconies of Simonas Petra now are trusted friends. I can only hope that this means my self-concern is losing its insistent voice. But that is more a hope than a certainty!

Arrived at Karyes, I once again went through the brief formalities, obtaining a *Diamonitirion,* this time for seven days. (The arrangements for a longer clearance had not materialized.) Then I went to try to discover how to get back down to Dafni in time for the 2 pm *caique* along the coast via Simonas Petra, Gregoriou, Dionysiou, and St. Paul – a trip that ends at the ancient *Skete* of St. Anne, near the tip of the peninsula, and not far from Karoulia – the 'desert' area where many of the more inaccessible hermitages are located.

KAROULIA

Cliff hermitages, Karoulia,
(Macedonian Heritage)

Karoulia, seen from a boat, which is the only way I have seen it, because it is 'rough country,' contains a quite unbelievable vertical community: small cottages and cells perched in the most improbable places on the cliff face, or on pinnacles of rock right out at the inhospitable, storm-beaten end of the Athos peninsula, where Xerxes had lost a fleet and twenty-thousand men before the time of Alexander.

A story is told by locals of the Russian Father Nikon mentioned before, who had been a nobleman in the Czar's court-and came to Athos after the revolution.

He spent six years in a cave on the Karoulia cliffs, with a vow never to speak to anyone. The story gets even stranger. When the six years were up, the first person he spoke to was a visiting Englishman, Gerald Palmer, who later headed the translation and publication of the *Philokalia* into the English language

Knowing that the human body replaces certain essential cells in twelve years, Father Nikon then decided to stay in Karoulia for another six years, so that in the end he would be *'made in Karoulia.'*

Demonstrating the strange mixture of dedication and humor that makes up the typical Athos character, this same Father Nikon, after the Second World War, asked English friends for a sweater. After some difficulty in that time of shortage, they finally found one, appropriately black, that had been made for Donald Campbell's speedboat racing team. The word '*Bluebird*' was embroidered boldly across the front.

Those who sent him the sweater carefully unpicked the name, imagining that monks' sweaters are universally undecorated. But when he finally received the sweater, he asked about the marks across the front. Told what they represented: *"Oh,"* he said, *"I wish you had left it."*

Repairing the Bus

When I had my papers, I went into the square from which the bus usually leaves. The bus was there, but the radiator was missing, and in front of the bonnet on the road lay a big, oily engine. Two men were working under the bonnet. I looked around until I found a traveler (German) who had a little English and a little Greek, and inquired. The bus was having a new-engine fitted, he told me, and would leave in about two hours ... just in time to catch the *caique*.

There came what seemed an enormously long wait, while, knowing the unreliability of 'timetable' information in those parts, I was afraid to leave the square for more than a few minutes at a time. Finally, in the bus, the new engine, which had been fitted but not yet connected-up when I arrived, started noisily, and a rush of final tests and adjustments began. Even then it was not time to go.

Once the adjustments were made, the driver and his assistant disappeared into one of the always-shuttered shops beside the square, leaving the engine roaring away. It was about an hour and a half before they finally emerged together, but in this time the new engine had obviously been 'run-in' as much as might be expected under the emergency conditions.

Half an hour later, seats and aisle packed with pilgrims who had by then been 'en route' in some way or other for five hours, and many of whom had yet to start their real journey on foot, the bus finally crawled out of the little town in its wooded valley, and up the steep slope that takes the dusty road over the hill and onto the steeper western side of the peninsula.

We passed a few small 'kellia' or houses, still then a mystery to me, although I knew that they normally contained two or three monks. These kellia house most of the working and administrative population of Karyes, including its twenty councilors, one representing each of the ruling monasteries. Then we passed an almost deserted, partly-ruined skete.

As the road became steeper and the sun hotter, I noticed the driver watching his temperature gauge. Finally, he pulled to a stop, turned round, and began to speak in Greek. All the dozen or so standing passengers packed into the aisle got out of the bus, and walked behind as he restarted. A slow and noisy half-mile later, when the road began to level-out before the long downslope to the coast, he pulled to a stop again and allowed his remaining passengers, who had kept up with the bus without difficulty, to re-embark. After that, it was 'all downhill' to Dafni, where we arrived after the midday boat from Ouranoupolis, and about twenty minutes before the caique was due to depart.

CHAPTER 9

PASCHA AT GREGORIOU

"It was revealed to Abba Anthony in the desert that there was one who was his equal in the city. He was a doctor by profession, and whatever he had beyond his needs he gave to the poor; and every day he sang the Trisagion with the angels." (From the *Gerontikon: Sayings of the Desert Fathers*)

Pilgrims in the courtyard (RA)

The quayside, normally quiet so early in the year, was packed with Paschal pilgrims visiting the different monasteries, and so was the little boat as it finally chugged out round the headland onto the slight swell and the colorful sea. Slowly, the great peak of Athos with its feather-of-cloud appeared behind the foothills. There it seemed for a while to move-out to meet us. And so I came, a little before three, to the jetty at Gregoriou, and up the shadowed slope, past the carpenter's shop with its rickety balconies, and into the main gate of the monastery.

105

I had heard that Lent in the monasteries was a difficult time. Now I found out what this meant. With the combination of the Lenten fast, the long services, and the need to make preparations for looking after sixty guests as well as for all the monks who had been away but would be returning to the monastery for Easter, some thirty or so monks had been preparing for a festival of some hundred and twenty people. No wonder many of them looked exhausted ... yet in a day or two, they were all-recovered, and their full qualities gradually became apparent.

But under these initial conditions, with large numbers of Greek-speaking pilgrims dominating the center of the stage, the differences in this different-world again caused enormous frictions within me: in spite of my invitation, I had at first trouble finding anyone to communicate with, trouble finding-out what was happening, trouble adapting to the food, trouble with the accommodation. I was given a bed in a room shared with four teenage Athenian pilgrims. They were pleasant enough, but so uncommitted that they slept in their room through the Easter services, and then talked and laughed for most of the night. The result for me was effectively a round-the-clock vigil with little real value in it.

Yet a few days later it had become difficult to see how I had found that initial adjustment so difficult: some things are so much of the body that they leave little trace in the memory. It was then that I began to understand that such frictions arise from any situation that conflicts with one's customary way of doing things, with one's *prolepses* – predispositions. The problem on Athos now is that the monasteries have been so flooded out with tourists and casual visitors that it has become difficult to establish communication, to attend the full range of services, or in any other way to pass beyond this phase of difficulty. This situation must in turn create for the monks the impression that all visitors are worldly or unstable. To this date, the situation continues to compound, so that it seemed that both the 'tourist problem' and the monks' doubts about the Western world continued to escalate.

Today, when we travel, we normally protect ourselves from all but the most minor frictions. Tourist hotels, unlike monasteries, earn their keep by helping us to preserve our own ways in foreign places. The better the protection, the higher the price! But on Athos, all my customs and habits – of timing, of diet, of rest and relaxation, and communication – all came under attack, and this created a great feeling of disorientation and loss of control.

At one point, when one of the monks in his haste seemed – if only because of my ignorance of Greek ways – to be manipulating me into a meaningless situation, a powerful fear was generated, and this for a while created its own secondary problems. Yet from the start, other things were going right, the beginnings of communication had obtained the Abbot's permission for me to attend services in the narthex instead of the porch of the church. When the candles were given out by the *Hegumenos* (Abbot) during the Easter service, he specially told one of the monks to bring me into the nave, where this ceremony was held, and himself gave me my Paschal candle.

It was after this, with the constant repetitions of: *"Christos anesti," "Alithos anesti." ("Christ is risen, He is risen indeed,")* sounding all-round, first in the church, and then through all that day and the following week all round the monastery, that I began to find communication opening up with the monks. But first, soon after the service, a young bearded pilgrim, a Cypriot whose English was good, told me that next day there would be a procession around the outside of the monastery, when the icons would be taken out to bless the grounds.

I had read that some of the Athonite abbots are famous for their addresses given after meals. Over the Easter period with its series of feasts, and its plethora of red hard-boiled eggs – made the more significant if we remember that, for many Greeks in the living past, eggs were available sometimes no more than two or three times a year. Now here they were available with and even between-meals.

Abbot George gave many such addresses. Unfortunately, I was unable to understand his Greek, although I could observe from the stillness and interest of his audience, as well as from his obviously skillful oratory, that his words were worth listening to.

In fact, I hoped later to be able to find out the gist of the message he had been telling, but this never happened. At the time, with a monastery full of Orthodox pilgrims, most of whom were only there on a long-weekend, he was too busy to talk to me.

On St. George's day – his 'name-day' – there was a small celebration. First, he invited all the fathers to his reception room on the ground floor of the guest-house. Later, we guests were invited to a similar small gathering. The room was large, about forty feet by fifteen, with seats all round the walls, and a cushioned wooden armchair at the head. The Abbot sat, and refreshments were offered all round. Then he spoke to me briefly, in quite good English.

Perhaps, I hoped, this would be my chance to learn his theme of that Easter. But it was not to be. After a few words for me in English, he continued entirely in Greek for the next hour or so. I learned later that most of those he was talking to were trade-unionists from Athens, many of whom had kept apart from the church, but were now beginning to question again.

MAKING FRIENDS

Communication then improved for me, because at this time I was introduced to one of the monastery's English speaking monks, Father P, a kindly young man who had then been at the monastery, if I remember correctly, for about three years. At our first short conversation, he told me that since the better English speakers were not there, he would try to help me. He came up to me again on the next evening, and suggested a walk.

This really was the beginning of my communication with the brotherhood. The worries and strains of the past few days fell away as if by magic, showing me clearly that what stopped me getting to know Athos is the 'hedge' of my own habitual reactions. Once through this hedge, the Holy Mountain is quite a different place, but this imaginary-mountain inside oneself must be climbed first.

Father P was born in Athens, and had studied for some months in England, which was how we could communicate. He was a graduate chemist.

He had spent some time in the monastery translating the stories of the Desert Fathers into modern Greek, before he had been 'promoted' to his job in the gardens.

Whenever the rigors of monastic life caused me problems, he went out of the way to help, yet did so in ways that did not spoil my wish to fit in as well as I was able – not always perfectly – with the monastic rule. He had a broad sense of humor ... something common among the monks there. He also had a wide understanding that came through in our long and valuable conversations.

For example, talking about the idea of the Orthodox equivalent of what some people call the 'way of the householder,' he told me that there are sometimes laymen in the world who are the equivalent of monks in their lives. These are the Dikaioi, the Righteous or 'Just' men described in the Bible. They put God first in their hearts. Their lives are outwardly the same as everyone else. Only 'by their fruits' can you know them. If they express the original form of the idea of *'justification by faith,'* then this idea must at one time have related to much more practical and visible changes in people than is normally observable today.

THE DIKAIOS

The Just Man, the *'dikaios,'* Father A told me, lives the simple life. His *metanoia* is internal, unseen by others. He follows the main virtues of the monk's life, yet may have an ordinary job and family-responsibilities. His renunciation is inner, not external, not visible ... but nonetheless real. He shares the virtues of the Christian monk: Each day and every day he dies to his own wishes and desires and does instead what God wants. Sometimes, this simply means that, without *'impertinent preferences,'* he does what is set before him.

> *"He is like the monk, because he resists the three temptations resisted by Christ on the mountain, when he was taken into the Desert to be tempted of the devil.*

The Just Man, like the monk, and like Christ when he refused to command that stones be made into bread for his comfort, resists desires and passions and the demands of the flesh by some form of asceticism ... often nothing more than acquiring the habit of saying 'no' to selfish demands ... but he begins this by acquiring the confidence that he can say 'no' to these demands. " (The monk Fr. P, in Gregoriou)

Our ability to resist temptation not only depends on our wanting to resist, but on our believing it to be possible. It is the desiring part of us that must be convinced. Sometimes, to convince it requires massive efforts.

MULES

Loading the mule (RA)

At other times, other ways are found. An Indian story illustrates this process:

An old woodcutter was in the habit of bringing his mules back from the river where he watered them. Outside his home he would bend down and pretend to hobble them. One day he became ill, and told his son to water the mules. In the morning, they were gone. "Did you hobble them?" asked the old man. "No," said the son, defensively, "you only pretend to do so, anyway." "But when I do so, they think they are hobbled," explained the old man.

I had a strange two-stage demonstration of the truth of this story at Gregoriou. At this monastery, mules used a passage under the muleteer's house down by the jetty. At one end of this passage, there is a single wooden rail, slotted into a hole in the stones on one side of the passage; it is normally simply rested on a step on the other side.

I immediately jumped to the conclusion that the mules were so intelligent that, if they saw the fence, they would not try to push it. I explained my conclusion to Father A. *"No,"* he said, *"it is to stop them getting into the passage during the day."*

It was I, and not the mules, who was 'misled by my intelligence.' I, who had made assumptions from what I had seen. It was my behavior, and not that of the mules, which provided the example I needed! Nevertheless, I had that example, the evidence that the mind is easily-blinded by its own conclusions. Thinking we know, we stop trying, then we stop investigating, and so we stop learning.

Perhaps this explains the strange psychological fact that clever people often cannot understand religion.

MORE ABOUT DIKAIOS

Father A had more to say about the *dikaios*.

"The dikaios resists the desire for fame. Christ refused to be tempted to cast himself down, to be caught up by the angels, and thereby gain glory in men's eyes. The Just-Man, the dikaios, also resists temptation. Often he must resist the temptation of earning money for the sake of money."

St. Irenaeus says that because Abraham believed God, he was considered to be a just man. This connects with Origen's idea of son-ship quoted elsewhere in this book: that only the son knows what is in the father's mind. This develops the Pauline idea of Justification by Faith, not as an abstract thing, but as a real and significant change in being and behavior ... a total reversal of our will.

"... not the spirit of the world, but the spirit which is of God."

As must be clear from the earlier chapters of this book, in spite of the difference between the monk's life and the forms of spirituality possible to man under modern conditions, the difficulties of Athos can form a kind of parable for the state of modern man; a parable in which we have chosen one kind of life, and the monks of Athos have chosen another. By choosing our life we choose what we experience of life, and this way we choose our memories.

Paradoxically, I discovered, it is only by giving up what we normally see as our precious freedom of choice that we can genuinely make free choices.

One of the great 'secrets' of monasticism is this fact that obedience leads to freedom. Pilgrimage, then, gives us new memories or makes certain memories more accessible to us. This changes us. On Athos, the monks have memories very different from the ordinary Western man.

Even for the pilgrim, the intensity (which is the measure of its attentiveness) of this Athos experience begins to create a different view of – and a different attitude and response to – the world.

THE FULCRUM OF THE WORLD

"Do you not know that in a race all the runners run, but only one receives the prize? So run that you may obtain it."
(I Corinthians 9:24)

On Athos, the main difference lies in the asceticism. Asceticism is practice. One basic idea of asceticism is explained in the words of St. Thalassios:

"Keep your body under control, and practice constantly; in this way you will soon be free from the thoughts that arise from your prolepses." (St. Thalassios, quoted in *The Philokalia: The Complete Text)*

This is the monk's method. He finds freedom from his predispositions by obeying a rule that changes those predispositions. If he is sufficiently sincere, his asceticism can, in-time, completely weed out the old, selfish predispositions.

The pilgrim, on the other hand, has only enough time on his pilgrimage to begin to lay down a few new and more spiritual predispositions: to make a small clearing in the jungle of his mind against the monk's possibility of achieving complete clearance. But in achieving this first clearance, I discovered, the pilgrim can also learn the need for some kind of rule, some kind of self-control of his own. In this time, the pilgrim who watches himself discovers that the modern idea of freedom of choice is no more than *'freedom to respond to temptation.'*

Of course, a kind of illusion operates; a delusion in which we normally consider that such a choice is true freedom, although in most of us, these choices are determined by external forces. The early fathers spoke of *synkatathesis* – which is voluntary assent to temptation. This is perhaps the origin of the legend of Mount Athos as *'the Fulcrum of the World.'* A film about Athos enlarges on this idea. *"There is a Jewish legend,"* states the commentator, *"which says that the survival of the world is assured as long as there remain thirty-six righteous men. 'Are you the righteous who preserve the world?,'* you ask the monk. *'Yes, replies the monk, yes!'"* (From the film, *"A Thousand Years Are as One Day."*)

Sometimes the monks speak of a legend in which there are seven, or sometimes twelve – (who's counting?) *'invisible gerontes'* on Athos. When one of them dies, another one is found. We have to learn not to take such legends too exactly, then we may understand what truths they convey.

When a theology of experience uses physical-images to explain non-physical truths, to understand this legend, and to understand the monks who live by it, we need first to share something of the memories of the monks, the black-robed men of Athos who remember and live by something that the West has forgotten. The monk knows things that do not pass our modern scientific 'tests' for truth, although they can be experienced: he knows things that are almost out-of-reach of experiment, yet leave men visibly changed. Such things are not new to this Grecian world, in which the human character has never been fixed as rigidly as in the English speaking Countries.

Homer described how the Argonauts, somewhere near Athos on their voyage, visited the Eleusian mysteries. When they returned to the ship, their faces shone. After two weeks or so, the shine had gone, but *"they remained changed men."*

GARDEN OF PANAGIA

Athos today is the Christian successor to Eleusis, here too are *Mysteria,* for here sacrament is experience, not merely symbol, and many of one's experiences become sacramental. But the concept of the *dikaios* is not subject to change.

Its meaning has been known since the time of Homer. It refers to an irreversible change in human nature and, in its full sense, to a discontinuous change ... a change now so rare that science has not yet described it. How can you investigate by controlled experiment somebody you cannot identify or control?

Its ability to produce such 'rare blooms' is one of the meanings contained in the statement that Athos is *'Perivoli tis Panaghia:'* the garden of the 'All Holy Virgin.'

CHAPTER 10

HEGUMENOS: AN ATHOS ABBOT

"The characteristic of the monk who lives in repentance is his attribution of every good thing to God. Depending on divine grace for everything, he has been stripped of every human wish to please himself." (Father George, Abbot of Gregoriou, in an address.)

It must be clear by now that a journey into Athos is – or can-be – much more than merely a journey into remarkable scenery or historic buildings. A journey into Athos can be a journey into a forgotten kind of faith: a faith which moves hearts at least, and perhaps moves mountains. My journey into Athos was a personal attempt to learn about this different kind of faith.

First, one obtains glimpses from the ordinary people who live near the Holy Mountain, from the monks, and from pilgrims who have been there before.

At first it seems almost naive. *"Strange things happen around Mount Athos,"* all these people will tell you. Yet one slowly discovers that faith on Mount Athos is very often far from blind-faith or superstition. It is, instead, closely associated with the ability to live with and accept the uncertainties of life. But it is more even than this. It involves a particular kind of acceptance and, supported as it is with prayer and worship, something is added to life that is not explained simply by our modern idea of acceptance. If there is something more to this faith than to blind faith, there is also something more to it than mere acceptance. Indeed, it is the ordinary form of acceptance of uncertainty which, wherever the spiritual life has decayed, wherever spiritual experience is absent, degenerates into blind faith and fatalism.

All this relates to the fact that the true Athos experience of faith, the true Christian experience, is not a merely intellectual change in belief, it is a change in attitude. This is a true *'change of heart,'* that begins with *metanoia,* seen as a change in the purpose from which one's life is motivated. This acceptance of uncertainty is one part of a great change in our inner response to life, in our living-relationship with the world in which we live. This change has been described by other sources as a change in the direction from which one's life is motivated; a change which shifts the center of one's being, at least in intention, from one's small self to God Himself. It is thus much more than merely a shift of priorities.

This involves a change in the movement of energy within-one, and also in the way the mind and brain function together, unlocking what might be figuratively called the *'door of the heart'* ... that sleeping part of the mind which is almost forgotten by modern man, but which is still remembered on Athos. When this door opens, I understand, one begins occasionally, perhaps for the first time, to be consciously, knowingly, guided and fed by what the Orthodox Christian knows as the Holy Spirit. We take our willfulness out of the way, and then the door is open; but only when we remember to *'keep a guard over our heart.'*

For me, the nature of the change was from dependence on externals to an Athonite dependence on God. This was encapsulated and demonstrated in what happened at the beginning of my seventh visit to the Holy Mountain. This is the story begun twenty pages back of a particular visit to Athos that in an external sense, started very badly, but in the strangest way it turned out very well indeed. As suggested earlier, the trip began badly because I learned at very short notice of a major business project that would tie me up for most of the autumn. How then would I get to Greece for my autumn visit to the Holy Mountain; by now, to me, an essential restorative? The project was to begin in about fourteen days time. When this news came, we began immediately making inquiries about flights. This flight was full, that hotel was full.

Eventually, however, we were able to arrange flights to take me there for a single week – actually seven-nights, with only six-days in Greece. But still, I would have no time to get the required 'passport' to the Holy Mountain. How this would be resolved, I had no idea. Perhaps I sensed that this was one of those tests of faith mentioned earlier. In any case, I flew, as they say, 'on a wing and a prayer!'

FATHER GEORGE AT KYRIA FANI'S

My wife and I arrived about 6 pm in Ouranoupolis, the gateway to Athos, and walked up to the house on the waterfront where we intended to stay. As we arrived, the door opened. Inside it, as well as the owner, were two black-clad, bearded monks, by then on their feet ready to leave.

For a moment I did not register our good fortune, then, with great delight I recognized them. There, with Father G, one of the priests of his *synodia*, was a smiling Abbot George of Gregoriou, whose monks had by then become such good friends of mine. I doubt he visits that house more than once a year or so, but on the next day, he was to take a memorial service in the nearby fishing village of Nea Rhoda, in order to comfort the family of a *caique* skipper who had died suddenly forty-days before. (His *caique* was one of the two providing daily ferry services to Gregoriou monastery, far down the coast of the Athos peninsula.)

Now, as we arrived, they were leaving the vine-covered house for the village church of Ouranoupolis, where, within minutes, they were to lead another service, that of *'blessing of the waters.'* More important, Fani, the owner of the house, had already told the Abbot of our problems. *"I have heard of your difficulties,"* he said immediately, *"I will be back on Monday, and then we will telephone the Governor together and see what we can arrange."*

We quickly got our bags into the house, had a quick wash, and set out past wind-blown acacia trees and the occasional houses, converted into shops, for the nearby village church. We arrived some minutes behind the two monks. For the moment, the important fact is that this journey to the mountain did not end here.

The promised telephone call on Monday produced an uncertain reply. Perhaps instructions would reach the local harbor police, perhaps not. Another telephone call, half an hour later, produced no reply from the police. Finally, as the minute for departure of the ferry approached, the Abbot said to me; *"Come, we see what we can do."* I grabbed my bag, and followed him down the road to the jetty, where he went straight to the policeman checking passports, and spoke softly to him. The port policeman, in his white naval uniform, looked at me, nodded to the Abbot, and then, looking at me again, inclined his head. I could go.

BURNING BUSH

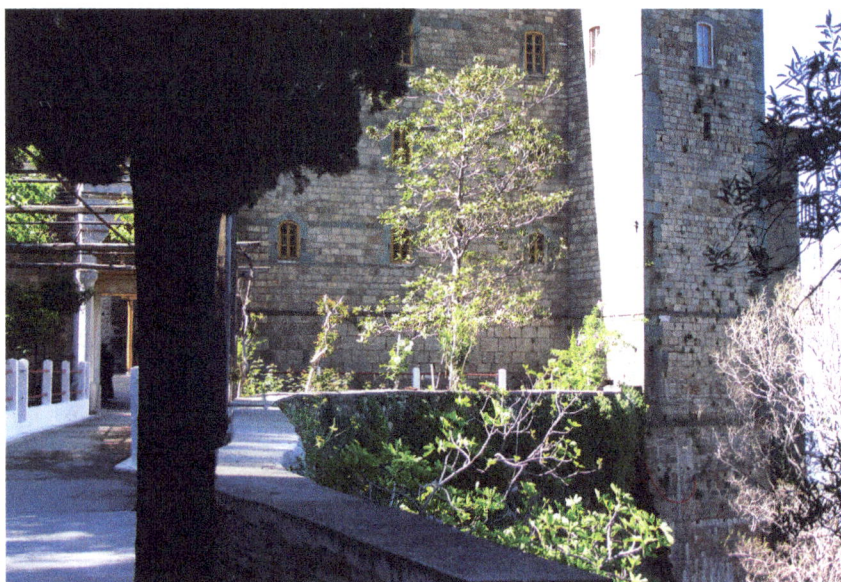

Monastery of Gregoriou (RA)

After reaching Gregoriou, I had a number of interesting and revealing conversations with Father A. One of particular importance was in the reception-room of the monastery guest house. He first showed me an icon of the Virgin on the wall. On this icon, he explained, around the Virgin the major prophets were shown, each to illustrate the particular aspect of their story in a way which helped to explain the 'inner' meaning of the birth of Christ. There was Jacob with his ladder, Moses with the burning-bush.

118

Something about this analogy fell into place. A strange experience that happened to me on a Christmas Eve many years before was lit up for me, and fitted into its Biblical context. The link between the Old Testament image of the burning-bush and the birth of Christ helped to explain this past experience, so I understood it better.

1 can only say that this made clear to me that fact that it is the forces existing in our unpurified minds – our fears and wishes, delusions and compulsions – which prevent the birth of Christ within our consciousness. Without the wedding garment of purity, without being free from these compulsions, we cannot be invited to the wedding.

Even more, according to a description by Evagrius, quoted in the *Philokalia*, it is the *logoi* – the 'inner essences,' the higher and more subtle impressions in the 'inner garden' of the mind – which need to be purified and ordered. So I asked myself, do these, when properly prepared, form the *'wedding garment'* of those who become saved? How can one answer such abstruse questions? In my state of mind, after a week on Athos, it seems to be so, yet after a few months in commercial England, such things no longer seem even 'reasonable.' Does anybody in the West today know clearly about such things? As I began to formulate these questions, the talk moved on to the discussion of experiences. Stillness, the emotional-stillness of *'hesychia,'* seemed very important.

During one of the services, one of the younger monks had showed me, without words, how many of those who are not in the chanting sit at the back of the church, repeating the Jesus prayer. Implicit in this was the idea that I might do the same.

CONCENTRATION

In support of this, Father A mentioned on another occasion how they had a high opinion of the spirituality of one Western visitor, because when they spoke to him while he was praying, he did not hear them speaking … very reminiscent of the Indian parable of the *'Arrow Maker'* who, while putting the point on an arrow, never noticed a wedding procession that passed in the street in front of him.

This kind of concentration seems to be much valued on the Holy Mountain. It depends on our finding inner-stillness, the '*peace that passeth understanding*' (Philippians 4:7), that is to say, a peace that is more than simply 'peace of mind.'

This peace does not depend on external or physical factors. This was confirmed by one remarkable experience that had happened to this kindly and erudite monk when, on an early visit to the monastery, an experience had actually led to his becoming a monk, Father A told me. Later, he took the 'Great Schema' (*megaloschema*), the more onerous rule that involved 1024 prostrations every day and 1200 repetitions of the Jesus prayer. This, I suspect, is as exacting and as precisely designed as Patanjali's eight-fold Yoga.

In it, he had another significant experience of a sudden influx of energy ... absolutely cold and still. He has since discussed this with other monks to whom the same thing occurred ... as it did to me the first time the *Hegumenos* (Abbot) blessed me.

Stranger still, when I returned to England, where I was being treated by an acupuncturist, immediately he had tested my pulses in their special way, I was questioned about the enormous amount of energy I had obtained from somewhere. Unfortunately, he then redistributed the energy, using a needle in what the acupuncturists call the 'alarm point,' and in the process, seemed to weaken my inner-development for some time to come.

SIDE CHAPEL LITURGY

It was at this point in my discussion that I asked Father A if I could take communion, which for an outsider requires the *geron's* permission, and next day, Father A took me aside after Matins, and before the beginning of the morning Liturgy. We went along the hall of the monastery guest house, and into one of many tiny chapels that exist around the monastery. Several familiar faces awaited me; monks who had been my friends since that momentous second visit two years before when I had first really made contact with them as friend rather than as puzzled visitor. With my old friend Father M as priest, I joined in the liturgy as best I could, saying the Lord's Prayer in English at the appropriate point.

Once again I had come home to Athos. *"Treat the monastery as your home,"* one of the monks told me later, as indeed they had said on previous visits. Tears arose unbidden, as the liturgy carried us toward the Kingdom. On the same visit, I remember talking about how one might help other people ... as well as about the question of how to live in the world and at the same time to serve God. Father A was quite firm about this. *"Don't bother too much about what to do,"* he told me. *"Get yourself right with God. The Just Man (the dikaios) is right with God, and that is how he can help. Then, wherever he is, people will find him and come for help."* Good advice, wonderfully good, but wonderfully difficult to carry out. Perhaps even more difficult back in England, in a world which is always 'doing,' so that we continually imagine ourselves to be *'deciding what to do.'*

Chapel Frescos in the Monastery of Gregoriou (RA)

CHAPTER 11

Metanoia: repentance

"When the monk possesses the grace of repentance, he knows the true God, and not some idea of God." (Father George, Abbot of Gregoriou, in an address)

Without remembering, repentance is incomplete. One of the saints likened it to a 'headless-axe.' Thus the idea that we must remember God is central to Athonite Christianity. To me, the reason why this is so is reasonably clear: it is only when I remember in the right way, with the heart, and not simply in my head, that something important and very desirable happens to me. Then, all that is personal and trivial falls away. It is then that I discover, all too briefly, a new clarity, a new breadth, a new peace. To paraphrase it: 'remembering means re-membering: re-connecting oneself inside.'

But more than this, in some strange way, what I obtain for myself in moments of remembering becomes the spring, the source of unselfish actions. When we are able to see ourselves without the normal pride, the normal conceit in our own superiority, we will see that without the 'Mary' of *metanoia,* the 'Martha' of our charity retains a taint of selfishness that spoils the whole. All my charity, ultimately all true charity, is founded on or inspired by this remembering; but whenever we 'forget,' we have also forgotten the importance of this remembering.

On Athos, then, *Mneme Theou,* remembering God, means something more than the 'subjective.' 'Objectively,' if one can say that, it means reconnecting oneself to God and His grace. The effort, the process involved, is very like that needed to remember a forgotten fact. It too sometimes succeeds, and sometimes fails. It succeeds, paradoxically, when we 'forget ourselves,' which means forgetting our ordinary thoughts, our ordinary motives, our insistent but very personal hopes and fears.

Then, when it fully succeeds, it connects us not only to something past, to some memory of something which once happened, but it also connects us more strongly to something existing in that moment.

As described in the parable of the *'Prodigal Son,'* this 'remembering' is all that God asks of us. We must: *"Seek first God's Kingdom"* (Matthew 6:33), and if we do this, He will do everything else that we need. So what is involved is 'to remember with the heart.' For most of us, remembering with the heart is not as easy as it should be. Yet the benefit it produces can be persistent if the effort is persistent. When we remember, something important changes within us. Then, we no longer act out of habit, out of our *prolepses*, the predispositions built up over a lifetime. When we remember, we act from a different kind of will.

But for this, we must wish in the right way, and usually our wishing, shaped by the past, is based on what the monk would call 'worldly pleasures,' for – again: *"Where your treasure is, there will your heart be also."* (Matthew 6: 21)

We think most of what we love most. So, to help us overcome our own past, places like Athos provide us with the tools we need to help us remember the best, tools to help us love.

GARDENER'S COTTAGE

Monastery gate (MG)

That evening, Father P and I walked out through the monastery gate, along the roadway crossed by vines, which overlooked the little harbor, then up the steps that form the beginning of the precipitous mule track to Dionysiou, the next monastery along the coast.

Walking slowly up the track alongside the back wall of the monastery, Father P explained to me that the next morning's service would include the procession I had been told about. In it, the icons would be carried round the monastery grounds and into the gardens in order to bless the whole 'estate.' At the same time, the icons would themselves be blessed in the traditional Athos manner. Then he showed me the route that would be taken on the morrow.

We followed this route up the steps to the gardener's cottage above and behind the monastery, and said that if I wished we might stop there for some refreshment, and perhaps even a little talk. After brief introductions, one of the monks then living in this whitewashed cottage with its vine covered terrace – Father A – seated me at the small table, and happily brought out an enormous tin of biscuits.

They were from his aunt, I was told. She was continually sending him gifts. *"Before I came to the monastery,"* he said, piling biscuits in front of me, *"she had one nephew. Now she says she has sixty."* (There were then about sixty monks at Gregoriou.)

Next, he made coffee, thick and sweet, with a small glass of raki. Father A is the monk in his thirties written about above, with whom I have become very close in my many stays in the monastery since our first meeting.

When I first met him he was, as I have already said, one of two gardeners living outside the monastery in the gardeners' cottage. This tiny whitewashed cottage, exposed to the winds on a hump on the mountainside immediately above the monastery, was only a hundred yards uphill from the monastery's single gate, and has its own small chapel as well as a simple kitchen. This first long discussion was exploratory on both sides.

Father P, Father A and myself sat on wooden chairs around a round oak table in the whitewashed hall of the cottage, with glass windowed doors at either end open to the evening breeze.

The monks were trying to discover how much I could understand, and I at the same time was trying to learn what they were able to understand; the type of intelligent, in-depth, exploratory conversation that I have found to have become more and more rare in England, where everyone nowadays is trying to make their own point.

The important thing in such exploratory discussions is quite different; the purpose is to find out how much common-understanding you share with another person. Once this is clear, communication becomes easier. In this case, I believe both 'sides' were delighted by the great agreement we found, and some hard-work was done on the establishment of a common language.

This process is a part of what I have learned to know as *'theological language,'* the flexible, sometimes a-logical language used to discuss one's experience of spiritual life. The decay of this mutable *'theological language'* into modern humanistic language, in which the same words have new and changing meanings alongside more rigid interrelationships, is probably the primary cause of decay in theology and philosophy in the West today. We do not allow the time necessary for older forms of verbal communication.

I don't remember all that was said. Much of it was not very significant except in the exploratory context of that particular conversation. It defined our common-ground and common-vocabulary, and part of it was their asking me questions about life in England at the present time. The monks at Gregoriou – as I myself – seemed then very concerned on the question of how the Western world has gone wrong. In support of my idea about language, they consider that one of the causes is that we intellectualize too much ... although to be honest, it would not be fair to say that the younger monks are entirely free of this taint.

This searching inquiry about life elsewhere was so often repeated on that visit, that it seemed at the time to be a general practice, at least in that monastery. But there was also more serious talk. We were talking about repentance, echoing the previous chapters about the need to turn away from one's habitual behavior, to go beyond one's predispositions. It was then that Father P first mentioned the word *metanoia*.

125

This was change of *nous*, they told me. Change of a higher part of mind. *Metanoia* involved redirecting this *nous*, which was more difficult.

My memory is a little hazy about this early conversation, so I may be adding too much of my own at this point, but there was little doubt that we understood much the same things, though initially in very different words.

It became more clear that in *metanoia* the *nous*, or non-verbal part of the mind, must turn towards God, a process described in the following passage:

"If with the help of Jesus we instantly quell a thought, we will avoid its corresponding outward action. We will enrich ourselves with the sweetness of divine knowledge, and so will find God, Who is everywhere. Holding the mirror of the nous firmly towards God, we will be illumined constantly as pure glass is by the sun. Then the nous, having reached the term of its desires, will in Him cease from all other contemplation." (St. Hesychios the Priest, quoted in *The Philokalia: The Complete Text*)

As I said earlier, *metanoia* is one of a number of ideas from the *Philokalia,* which without knowledge of the writings of the Early Fathers, is very easily misunderstood, as it can be understood only by putting it into practice. Even then, its true meaning is sometimes forgotten when we are not in a right state.

Metanoia can be seen in three ways. It is a stage to be reached, a decision to be made, to repent of one's life and to begin striving to find a new direction for that life. Once that striving has been begun, repentance is also something that has to be repeatedly done. Repeatedly, we are drawn towards the world, and repeatedly we turn again to God: *"This is a monk's life. I fall down, and I get up again. I fall down, and I get up again."* (From the film about Athos, "A Thousand Years Are as One Day.")

Katholikon (main church) seen from above (RA)

This is symbolized by the one thousand and twenty-four prostrations made every day by hundreds of monks of the *Megaloschema,* each time repeating the Jesus prayer.

This internal falling and rising again is also the life of all those who make the same kind of decision while remaining *'in life,'* as some do, even today.

In this case, it has no outward symbol, but as a result, it is even more important to continually be watchful, as without watchfulness it is impossible to turn inward repeatedly.

When misunderstood, this is easily assumed to be something merely external ... Such 'incomplete *metanoia'* was likened by the early fathers to a headless-axe because *metanoia* misunderstood no longer 'cuts' between *nous* and the ordinary, dianoetic mind. Full understanding of this idea is expressed in the passage from St. Hesychios quoted earlier. It seems as if, from complete *metanoia,* the mind less often returns to its old ways.

The whole process is described in the parable of the *'Pearl of Great Price'* (Matthew 13: 45 – 46). The importance of *metanoia* is also symbolized, at least in the writings of St. Neilos, by the wood of the cross, by which Jesus was lifted-up while being killed. The opposite of this is symbolized in the Old Testament, where Lot's wife looked back and became a pillar of salt. As long as we are turned to the outward world, we remain unaware of the sweetness of God.

Yet *metanoia* is not a bitter repentance. In St. Gregory of Nyssa, the immediate reaction after a monk's renunciation is symbolized by the bitter waters found by the Israelites on their escape from Egypt, but, he says there, *"the water turned sweet when the wood of the cross was immersed in it."* This is true *metanoia.*

The idea of *metanoia* was explained in a more practical way in a later talk with Abbot George, during the only full day I had in the monastery during my seventh visit.

On that Tuesday morning, just after returning from the memorial service he had taken in the fishing village of Nea Roda, he came into the Katholikon during Matins. As the service proceeded, there came a time when all the monks came up to him one by one, touched the floor and kissed his hand. Then the few laymen present joined the line. Without being prompted, I did the same, happy to be able to show my respect and affection for this wise and kindly man.

The service continued, Matins came to an end, and the priests and deacons of the monastery lined up in the small ritual that precedes the liturgy. The Abbot remained in his stall, and indeed, on this day, I don't remember all that was said. Much of it was followed by a scattering of monks to different chapels. It was a little while before I understood. Because the Abbot had been absent on the Sunday, everyone would take communion together on the Tuesday, instead of on Sunday. Happily, I venerated the icons after the monks, and took my communion with the rest.

After the service came the morning meal: small fish fried in a light coating of flour, bread, a small chocolate-sweetmeat wrapped in foil, a plate of fruit, small peaches, an apple, grapes from the monastery vineyards.

During the meal, Father A came up to me to say that he would not be able to talk to me that morning as planned: he had to go to Karyes, and then to the monasteries of Ivirion and Stavronikita.

As he would not be back before I had to leave, he would ask Father P to talk with me instead.

The meal ended, and I returned to tidy my room. After a while, I took a book and went out through the inner gate, through the tunnel-like outer gateway, with its seats on either side and its great iron-bound gates propped open. I found my favorite seat by the pine-tree overlooking the little harbor, and settled to absorb the impressions of the day and its long service. I then began my self-imposed task for the visit of translating the little French book of quotations from St. Isaac the Syrian into English.

The monastery's work continued as usual. Above the sound of a distant fishing boat, I could hear the noise of mules and of monks working together down by the harbor. Birds squabbled in the bushes on the cliff below me. The almost-motionless sea stood, dark and royal, in the shadow of the land. After a while I heard voices coming down the road from the main gate. I looked round and saw the Abbot with several older monks. He was carrying his 'everyday' staff, an ordinary brown wooden staff but with two leaping fish carved at its head, a simple imitation of the great formal staff used on the major ceremonies of the monastery, so that it seemed he was making an official journey of inspection. As he passed me, he stopped and came towards me. I stood, again kissing his hand.

"I hope you are comfortable," he asked. I told him yes, and very happy to be there. *"Now I must go to the harbor,"* he continued, *"we will talk later, if that is alright"*

I thanked him, and he continued with his entourage, very much the feudal Christian lord in his own domain ... expressing ancient patterns of life that have barely existed for several centuries by now. An hour and a half later, he returned up the hill with two of the older monks.

"Would you like to come now?" he asked. I walked up the path with him as he called one of the monks to ask about some grapes that had fallen from the vine overhead. They had been trodden into the path.

Although my Greek is inadequate, I think from the tone that he said something mild, like: *"Shouldn't these have been cleared up?"* The response was clear and immediate, the monk addressed hurried off for brush and hose.

As we continued, I followed Father George as he crossed-himself in front of the icon over the gate, and so through, into the inner court, round behind the Katholikon, and so up the wooden staircase to the monastery's offices, and so to the Abbot's private office. After this, he came quickly to the point. What questions did I have to ask?

"It is really about prayer," I told him, *"I know in a sense what to do with the Jesus Prayer, but the question is, how to do it without my mind wandering. This seems to need a kind of feeling which I have when I am here, but which often is gradually lost when I leave here; an emotion which drains-away. The need to overcome this was what first brought me to Mount Athos and here to your monastery. It is not a question of 'doing,' but an emotional question that asks how we can want what we need?"*

The answer made it clear that this connects with our false self-will, our willfulness. Father George told me: *"This kind of feeling must come from God, from the Spirit. Yet even this does depend on our efforts. God can and sometimes does it without anything done on our part, but He wants our efforts, so more generally He gives it only when we make effort, and the efforts must also be of the right kind – efforts of repentance."*

It became clear that repentance, in Athonite terms, is, above-all, a transformation of emotion. To quote the address by Father George that I noted earlier, it is: *"a sanctified eroticism which strains towards the beloved Lord, a sign of profound humility and desire for God."*

St. Maximos the Confessor said about this that: *"At times Scripture refers to God as eros – desire – and at other times as agape – love, and at still other times as the desirable and the beloved. He Himself, as desire and as love, moves towards us while, as the desirable and the beloved, He moves all those creatures toward Himself who are capable of desiring and loving. It is thus that the great Apostle, St. Paul, having come into possession of divine-desire, and participating in its ecstatic power, cries out, inspired: 'I live,' he says, 'yet not I, but Christ lives in me.'*

He speaks as a lover, and, as he says himself, also as someone caught up in the ecstasy of God, and no longer living his own life, but instead, the life of the beloved, the beauty surpassing speech." (St. Maximos the Confessor)

All of this is to do with change of heart. As I have said before, this is more difficult to obtain, but more permanent than merely changing one's mind. Humility is an important element in this change. *"Humility is the key to Athonite Christianity,"* said the Abbot. *"Repentance: repenting of our willfulness, is the key to humility."*

Of course, like many other key Christian concepts, this whole idea of repentance has changed over the centuries in the West, and for the English-speaking reader it clearly needs clarifying. The clarification for me came first in the Abbot's answers to my questions. It was developed further by reading recent English translations of addresses he had given. *"Repentance"*, he wrote, *"is for what we have done in the past, which we feel is not quite right. Where we have confessed, or where we have truly repented, God afterwards takes the mistake, the sin, as not done-willingly, not with our will."* (*'Forgive our sins, voluntary and involuntar*y,' as the Orthodox liturgy puts it.) He next explained how true repentance must be emotional, not simply 'legalistic.' 'Lip service' is not enough.

THE YOGI AND THE MONK

The essentially Christian nature of this emotional component is described by a story Abbot George told me. This was about a conversation between a monk from Athos and a yogi from India. They were comparing the similarities and differences in their ways. This is how I remember this story:

"We have prayer," said the monk.

"We also have prayer," said the yogi, *"and we practice asceticism for hours, and even for years at a time."*

"We too are ascetics," replied the monk. *"We try to remember God at all times."*

"We too practice recollection," said the yogi, *"and we strive for repentance."*

The conversation went on for some time. The list grew longer and longer. Finally, the monk told the yogi that; *"We have compunction."*

"Compunction?" asked the yogi. *"We do not have compunction ... what is compunction?"*

Father George then continued: *"Repentance must be of the heart, so it must be followed by katanyxis: contrition or compunction."* (This was once described as 'remorse of conscience.')

"Yes," I put in at this point, *"This is exactly the difficulty; the difficulty is how to achieve this katanyxis, this emotional feeling of repentance. It comes, but it does not come often enough."*

"This too needs the help of the Spirit," Father George explained, making it clear that the obstacle was the familiar one, because our everyday willfulness is not a sufficient tool for the spiritual life. To waken our heart, something is needed more than the efforts of the ordinary verbal mind. *"You cannot develop it willfully, so you should pray often to God for it. Pray that He grants you katanyxis, this contrition."*

Once again, I was brought back to the key question of awakening or changing the heart. Head wakes every day. Superficial feelings awake with every casual impulse. But the spiritual heart is not so easy to awaken.

METAMELIA

To come back to my earlier conversation with Father A: after talking about metanoia, Father A said that there was another word that was equally important. This was *metameleia*. The other root in this word, *meleia*, seems to refer to the 'stream of consciousness' or association of ideas that goes on so continually in the modern mind.

Metameleia is the practice of transforming these individual activities when they become too insistent, as they so often do. Once again, it is a way of 'working on' and changing the ordinary mind. They also speak about making specific prayers to achieve this, to counteract specific habits: something I have since tried with some success.

The other thing I particularly remember about that visit, apart from the warmth of the welcome I received, and the joy of finding shared understanding, was the strange but pleasant raspberry-like cordial Father A unearthed from somewhere.

"I am well known for this," he said. *"I get it specially from Cyprus."* Very light and refreshing it was.

The day after my conversation in the gardeners' cottage, a procession formed about 7 am after a two-hour service in the monastery church. (Services are shorter immediately after Easter). Although some of the visiting laymen were by then collecting icons for the procession, I was still uncertain of things, and hung back until Father P came up to me. *"Do you want to join the procession?"* He asked. I said I did.

"Then come," he said.

We went into the narthex, and I was given an icon of one of the Athos saints, a writer of great spirituality. (Was it a coincidence, or was there method in this choice? The next day I was given a private room, and an icon of the same little known saint hung there.) In the early morning sunlight I joined the procession, carrying an icon, and guided by Father P, who was a great help in telling me where to go and what to do, as well as explaining things as they went along.

We walked slowly through the monastery, and then up the track behind, preceded by chanting monks: the Abbott with his staff with the two golden fish; priests in robes with staffs or censers; forty or fifty monks and laymen in all, each holding an icon in front of him. Finally, the procession reached the gardeners' cottage, where a series of short ceremonies was completed. Then we all filed onwards, past the Abbot's upraised hand, in a ceremony in which each person kissed the icon held by each of the others before, slowly, the procession returned to the shade of the monastery courtyard.

The day went well. After the service and the meal that followed, I spent some time sitting in silence overlooking the water.

I also talked for an hour with Father P on one of the balconies overhanging the sea, a conversation again given to answering questions about what was happening in England. Then I talked in the guest house kitchen for half an hour or so, and there was a monk drinking coffee who looked vaguely familiar. He spoke, apparently asking in Greek who I was, and remarking that he thought he had seen me before. He was Father M, I discovered, down for a brief visit from Simonas Petra. I had of course seen him there on my previous visit. We exchanged greetings, and I said that I expected to visit his monastery shortly.

"You will be welcome," he said, and smiled.

Father P also helped in my conversation with one of the older fathers, Father G. This father, perhaps about sixty, with a rich white beard, was Greek, and spoke no English. When I had been there about five days, he spoke to Father P in my presence.

"He wishes to know your name," Father P told me. I told him my name, and the two Fathers talked for a few moments. *"Father G wants to say,"* was the interpretation, *"that since you first came here he has felt a great love for you in his heart. He wants to know, do you have any family?"*

I explained. He wanted to know whether my family was in Greece with me. When I said that it was not possible to bring Nicholas, our son, because he was autistic, Father G paused for some time. Finally he spoke briefly.

"He says do not worry," was the translation, *"the boy's salvation is taken care of."* But how had he known that this, the question of salvation for our non-communicating child, was my wife's greatest worry? Almost always, when Athos answers questions, it creates new ones!

I think it was the following day that I left early for Simonas Petra, back along the coast towards Dafni, and much higher-up the mountain than Gregoriou.

It is *metanoia* and sacrament, not philosophy, that 'melts' the base metal of men's hearts, allowing them to take new form.

It is the Western cult of individuality and personality, and our 'attitude of doing,' which 'fixes' our character in an unchanging way even when it has no need to be fixed ... the Ice Queen's breath that turns men's hearts to easily-fragmented ice.

The Greek word, used before Plato, but still used by modern Greek thinkers today, is *'atomism,'* a term for the false *'I-it'* individuality, or false self-hood of predominantly selfish action that underlies the nature of Western thought and action. It is this which rules most of Western religion. In the West, this 'atomism' is now an ingrained element of the 'shared *prolepsis,'* built into our ideas, our attitudes and behavior. It fills our memories. Now that it is become habit, so it is very difficult to escape from it.

It has even crept into our prayers. I remember Father A on one occasion talking about prayer. He mentioned a book in English that talked about five stages of prayer. *"On Athos,"* he told me, *"they only recognize four of these stages; there is an added first stage, that of asking God for things, that is not considered to be true prayer."* (It is supposed to have been Turgenev who said that all prayer could be summed up as: *"Dear God, please make two and two not equal to four."* But this is also quite foreign to the Athonite view of prayer.)

On Athos, one discovers that what matters is a difference in attitude. Here there are monks, and even laymen, who lack this 'atomist' element in their thinking. They remember something that individuals of the West have forgotten ... a still small voice in the heart which speaks without words; a voice that demands flexibility, or gives purpose that can never quite be put into words.

"The force that through the green fuse drives the flower

Drives my green age"   (Dylan Thomas)

And who shall ask the flower for its reasons? Or demand of the monk his deepest motives? Sufficient that they are, for this is the question of being, the question that is meaningless to the head, and which heart alone can answer.

The heart does not know *'the how of things'*, but the *'why.'*

This is why the truths of the heart can only be affirmed, not explained.

CHAPTER 12

PHILOXENIA: HOSPITALITY

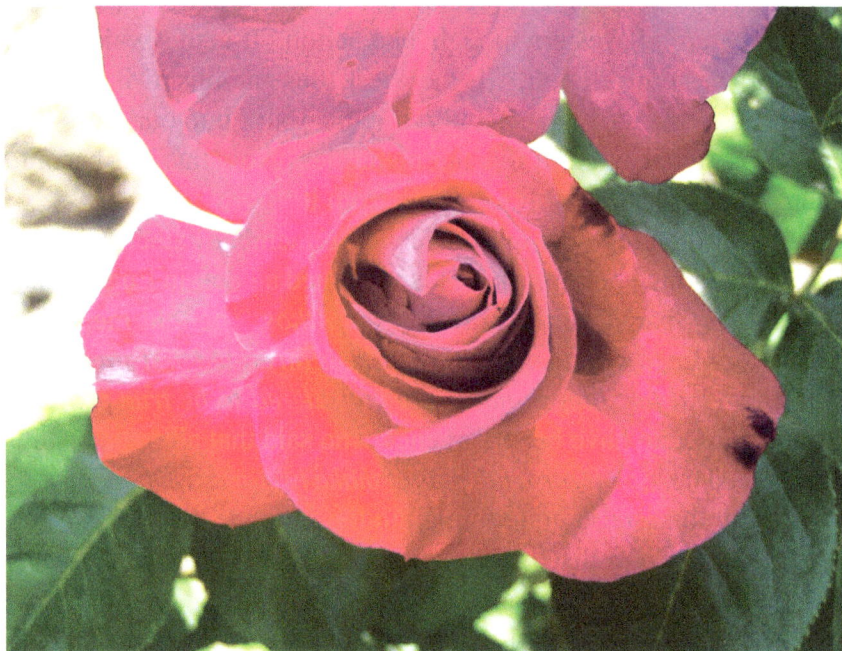

Rose from the monastery garden (MG)

Father A had been working on translating the 'Gerontikon' – the collected sayings of the elders of various early communities, from the 'patristic' Greek of the early fathers into modern Greek. The Gerontikon is, simply translated, 'the sayings of the old men (gerontes or elders).' From this Gerontikon, Father A told me the story of the man who made baskets in order to live.

Although very poor, he was renowned for always giving so much to charity. One day, this man made some baskets, then went into the town to sell them in the market.

As he was walking into town, he met a leper, and the leper said to him: *"Are you going into town?"*

"Yes," said the man. *"Then take me with you,"* the leper continued. The man carried both the baskets and the leper into town.

"Put me down beside you while you sell your baskets:" said the leper. So he put him down, and when he sold his first basket, the leper said: *"I need some food."*

So the money from that basket went to buy the leper some food. And so with the other baskets, to buy the leper fruit, meat, anything he needed. And at the end of the day, all the baskets were sold, and every drachma had been spent on the leper.

"Now," said the leper, *"you are going back my way. Please carry me back where you found me."* So the man did so. When they arrived, he gently laid the leper on the ground, when his burden was transfigured into an angel, who said: *"I have tested you, to learn if it was true what they said about you. It is true, and I give you great honor."*

PHILOXENIA AND HESYCHIA

According to the *Gerontikon,* I was told, the fathers consider that there are two ways for the monk: the way of withdrawal, of '*hesychiah*,' and the way of hospitality, '*philoxenia,*' which was the great Greek virtue until the tourists came.

The difference between these ways is described in a parable from one of the early fathers, who spoke of seeing in a dream two famous monks who had died. This is illustrated in a story also told in the *Gerontikon*: *"They tell the story of a certain brother who came to Scetis to see Abba Arsenius, and who went into the church and entreated the clergy to take him to see him and the clergy said unto him: 'Refresh thyself a little, and thou shalt see him.' And the brother said unto them, 'I will eat nothing before I meet him and see him;' and when the clergy heard this they sent a brother with him to shew him Abba Arsenius, because his cell was some distance away. And when they had arrived there, they knocked at the door and went inside, and having saluted him, and prayed, they sat down and held their peace; and the brother who was from the church answered and said, 'I will depart, pray ye for me.' But when the other brother saw that he possessed no freedom of speech with the old man, he said unto the brother from the church, 'I also will go with thee,' and they departed together.*

137

"Then he entreated him, saying, 'Take me also to Abba Moses, who was a thief,' and when they went to him, the old man received them with joy, and having refreshed them greatly, he dismissed them in peace. And the brother who had brought the visitor to Abba Moses said unto him, 'Behold, I brought thee to a man from a foreign land, and to an Egyptian, which of the two pleaseth thee?' And he answered and said unto him, 'The Egyptian who hath just received me and refreshed me.' And when one of the old men heard what had happened, he prayed to God, and said, 'O Lord, shew me this matter; one fleeth from the world for Thy Name's sake, and the other receiveth and is gracious for Thy Name's sake.' And behold, suddenly there appeared unto him on the river two great boats, and lo, Abba Arsenius and the Spirit of God were traveling in silence in the one, and Abba Moses and the angels of God were in the other, and they were feeding the monk with honey from the comb." (From the Wallis Budge translation.)

To the monk, the black Father Moses is the symbol of hospitality, and the other father a symbol of the Hesychast, who takes the way of the hermit and keeps himself apart from the world. Both ways have equal value, are of equal importance.

On Athos, I was told, many of the monasteries are dedicated to the way of hospitality. Gregoriou is dedicated to hospitality, but often seems to contain monks of both 'types.' Certainly, they are no foreigners to stillness of heart. The hermitages, particularly those on the rocky 'deserts' and cliff-sides of Karoulia, the lower slopes of the mountain itself, at the seaward end of the peninsula, are where many of the *hesychast* hermits live; those who wish to keep far from the world.

Father A then continued his explanation of the idea of his church, by saying that in the town of Volos, and in the villages around the slopes of the mountain Pelion, the church is as it should be, and the life of the villages is as it should be everywhere in Greece, if only it had not been spoiled by the growth of cities. He advised us, when we could, to go and look there. We later discovered that this was the one part of Greece not badly tyrannized by its Turkish conquerors, the only part of Greece, apart from Athos, where the old ways, many surviving from Byzantine times, still continue to this day.

It is therefore a place to observe these ways as they exist in ordinary community life.

On the subject of community and life, he wanted to know if we owned a garden. This, he said, was important. Sitting not in the gardener's cottage, but in the guest house kitchen of the monastery as I sipped a cup of fragrant local grown tea, or stood by the window, looking down on the heaving springtime sea far below, he continued. First, he suggested that everybody needs the experience of meeting their needs by their own labor, and so seeing how the things they need are obtained, often with the help of nature.

In some way, he suggested, people who lack this experience lack something essential. For example, the bread and wine of the Eucharist have little meaning to many city people. He commented that the pilgrims who come from far places to the Holy Mountain all seem to be aware of this, and almost-all have their own land, gaining understanding from its use. I find this view interesting, because it has seemed to me that for a long time our society in England was divided into those who understand the relation between work and the things they receive for their lives, and those who do not.

The Athos view is slightly different, because it places more emphasis on the fact that these things are provided by nature, and less on the effort needed to obtain them.

Father A – and perhaps all the fathers – seemed to be worried about two things: about Western ways of thought and their effects on society, and particularly on Greek society, and about the growth of cities. Athens, he said, now contains something like forty per cent of the entire population of Greece, and he sees the landless-life of cities as the great problem, perhaps the cause of all the problems in our modern society. It is as if many modern city-dwellers of that time – almost thirty years before this book was first written – had begun to think as-if the riches of the land provide themselves. I spoke with him about the psychological and economic pressures that drive people to the cities, particularly describing the economic pressures, and said that as yet I knew of no real alternative to this. Clearly, very great and traumatic changes, both in society and in individuals, would be needed before a real alternative became possible.

He asked me, what did the English Church believe about the sacrament of the Eucharist? I found this difficult to answer, and finally told him that each Anglican priest seemed to have his own opinions, and that this was one of the big problems in the way of England's religious-recovery.

He also tried – very hard – to help me understand certain of the underlying concepts behind the kind of Orthodoxy practiced on Athos. For example, he told me that a big festival outside the mountain had used singers who were professional, and ... *"more skilled than our singers in the church,"* he told me. *"Then the comment is made: why don't we get better trained singers? But we prefer voices which sing from love of God."* This echoes the following passage from 'The Art of Prayer,' which sets what we might find an impossibly high standard for today: *"... in order that the singing of Church songs may lead us on to be filled by the Spirit, the Apostle is insistent that the songs should be spiritual. By this it should be understood that they must be not only spiritual in content, but moved by the Spirit: they must themselves be the fruit of the Holy Spirit, and be poured forth by hearts that are filled with Him. Without this, they will not lead to our possession by the Spirit.*

"This is according to the law whereby 'the singer is given what he has put into the song.'

"The second condition of the Apostle is that songs must be sung not by the tongue only, but by the heart. It is necessary not only to understand the song, but to be in sympathy with it, to accept the contents of the song in the heart and to sing it as if it came from our own heart. A comparison of this text with others made it evident that in the time of the Apostles, only those who were in such a state would sing ..." (*The Art of Prayer,* Hegumenos Chariton of Valamo, Translated by Kadlubovsky and Palmer.)

FIELDS READY FOR HARVEST

We then had a brief discussion on the passage where Jesus says that: *"the fields are ready for harvest, we pray to the Lord of the harvest to send laborers to this harvest."* (Matthew 9:37-38)

He was, I think, referring to the difficulty of finding people qualified to help the many people drawn now to the mountain or searching for unchanging truth in a changing world.

I remarked that this quotation had meant a great deal to me for twenty years or more. But lately it had been difficult for me to carry on in that direction until I had put my own house in order again. In response to this, another of Father A's stories about Abba Moses was told, again of the black Father's hospitality: *"An order was given at Sketis: 'Fast this week.' Now it happened that some brothers came from Egypt to visit Abba Moses, and he cooked something for them. Seeing some smoke, the neighbors said to the ministers, 'Look, Moses has broken the commandment, and has cooked something in his cell.' The ministers said: 'When he comes, we will speak to him ourselves.'*

"When the Saturday came, since they knew Abba Moses' remarkable way of life, the ministers said to him, in front of everyone, 'O Abba Moses, you did not keep the commandment of men, but it was so that you might keep the commandment of God.'"

Hospitality, *philoxenia,* they say, is the law of God. The most common icon of the Trinity, the *'philoxenia'* icon which shows Abraham entertaining the three angels, clearly links this idea of *philoxenia* with *koinonia,* the undemanding love that Athonite theology tells us is the basis of the relation between the three persons of the Trinity.

On two occasions, Father A made this point by describing two frescoes that exist elsewhere in Greece. In one of them, *'heaven,'* all the people are eating, and each has, instead of a hand at the end of his right arm, a spoon, each feeding the other with his spoon.

In *'hell,'* they have the same 'spoon hands,' but each is striving to feed himself, and most of the food is dropped before it gets to their mouths.

Agape, says Abbott Vasileios of Stavronikita, is the true Christian relationship. By entering this relation of emotional sensitivity with those around us, we also enter the *koinonia* of the Trinity. This is the power of the new commandment.

The *philoxenia* icon shows the connection between the *koinonia* relationship and the sharing of the bread and wine in the liturgy. This is one of the few hints one can easily uncover about the liturgy itself, for the monks consider that experience, not explanation, is the best way to learn about the sacraments.

INVITATION TO RETURN

Although he took great care not to appear to act as a 'teacher' or instructor to me, on our last long conversation before I left, Father A gave an unintentional demonstration of the way the monastery expresses this idea of *philoxenia,* when he suggested I should try to come back to them 'after a while.'

"Many people come here to be refreshed, and then they carry something back to the community where they live," he told me, *"so they find they need to come back quite often. About three times a year seems right."*

This was an invitation to me from all the Fathers, he told me. He said that this constant flow from Athos to the communities around was the main reason for the existence of the monasteries.

Now this was involving more and more people from the West.

This echoed what he had said when I asked if he could spare the time to talk any more. *"It is my duty, my job,"* he told me. This also reminded me of something said by Father P on another occasion: *"If you were not here, there would be no reason for us to be here."*

Later on during my stay, I finally had my chance to talk directly to Abbot George. I say *'finally to talk directly,'* because it had for some time been obvious that somebody had been in part orchestrating my meetings and some of my brief conversations with the other monks. I had been told things, shown things, and tested, all to some kind of overall plan!

This conversation with the Abbot himself was most difficult to describe. Also, it was a disappointment to me, if only because I myself did not make enough use of what was obviously a valuable and privileged opportunity.

Abbot George, the *'geron'* and spiritual-father of Gregoriou monastery, is a very busy man. One night, when I was to see him, Father P first forewarned me and then called for me after the last service of the day, Vespers. As night was falling over the mountain, and the lights of the fishing boats shone over the Aegean, he guided me to a part of the monastery I had barely seen before, a long building behind the Katholikon. There he first of all showed me into a small chapel, and drew my *attention* to one elaborate icon. This showed Mary surrounded by many angels. There was a black river falling into a series of stone basins.

This too reflects experience. *"Theotokos as the source of life,"* he explained. He told me that the next day's service was in praise of the Mother of God *as the source of life.* I did not entirely understand, yet somewhere inside me, I gained from this encounter.

SOURCE OF LIFE ICON

Next, the young monk took me through into the Abbot's small office. There I was given a crystallized fruit and a glass of water, and then left for a few minutes to await the Abbot, who had been delayed. Finally, Father George arrived, greeted me warmly, and hoped my stay had been enjoyable.

I inquired after his health, and from his answer gained the opinion that perhaps he was too busy, had too many responsibilities. Of course, it was then the busiest time of the year in the Orthodox calendar. Abbott George's main interest in talking to me was to discover if my interest in Athos and what the mountain stands-for was longstanding and sincere, or was simply capricious.

He followed my interest back through various sources of information I had found in the past, until I came to mention Saint Silouan. When I mentioned that my interest in Athos had been awakened in the first place primarily by Silouan's own words, which I in some way recognized, he seemed to be satisfied, and left this line of inquiry.

I was there some fifteen minutes in all, perhaps too aware of the fact that the monastery's day would start so early the next morning. But before I left his office, he asked me if I had a prayer rope?

143

When I said that I did, he was pleased, and said that: *"the Jesus Prayer is the principal export of Mount Athos."*

FIRST BLESSING

I asked for his blessing, and received it. Of that, it is difficult to comment, although the memory of it lingers with me to this day, and by its reality a 'real' link was created, which will never pass. Finally, as I left, he called a monk to guide me across the dark courtyard.

The conversations and little object lessons continued through the following days. I have probably got them out of sequence in this account, because there were so many of them. But much of the meaning came to fruition at the end of my visit.

This, perhaps by coincidence, was the next time I had any close contact with my friend Father S. This was on my last morning, when he joined in the small liturgy in honor of St. Christopher – to which I was again invited. This service was held in the bright little whitewashed chapel of the garden cottage, with its simple varnished iconostasis and few icons. The congregation consisted of three monks, a priest, (who was also the normally taciturn guest-master of the monastery), and myself.

The service was followed by what I can only call a 'goodbye breakfast' in the simple, small, and rather dark kitchen of the cottage, which was in many ways like a self-contained little monastery.

On that occasion, Father S talked continually. Although some of what was said was translated for me, I don't remember it. On this occasion it seemed to consist largely of weak jokes.

"Don't worry," Father A commented, *"he always makes jokes when he is happy."*

I left with that strange sensation often described as a 'lump in the throat,' after one of the many emotionally moving experiences, which somehow occurred more often in the quietness of the mountain than in our more excitable English environment.

It is the older monks, like Father S, who in their simplicity most visibly demonstrated the emotional openness that is the characteristic of that monastery of Gregoriou.

Yet even the younger monks demonstrated clearly their obedience to the discipline of their lives, an obedience that appears sometimes as an inexplicable impersonality.

Earlier in my visit, I remember Father P telling me how he had first visited Mount Athos as a young man, just like the many young pilgrims who had come there over Easter. He had seen then the joy on the faces of the monks, and this had changed his view of life.

Although he said he only came to the monastery many years later, and for other reasons, this early experience was obviously of great importance in shaping the later decision. Confirming the earlier passage about the bitter waters and the pleasure of the liturgy, he said to me, while we were returning from the procession, that *"most of a monk's pleasures are spiritual ones."* This was most appropriate just after the end of the rigorous forty-days-fast for Lent. For a newcomer from a different culture, this different point of emotional balance was surprising.

Athos is a difficult place to take without discovering some conflict in one's mind. How is one to reconcile the love and happiness that exist on one level with the frictions and discomforts that arise on another? I must admit I myself have the greatest difficulty in giving a balanced view of my visits.

In addition, on this second visit and those that followed it, much of what was said and what happened was of too close and personal nature to repeat in a book like this ... another problem is the impossibility of doing in words anything like justice to the services, which were, among other things, such superb communication to all the senses at once.

This subtle communication often slips almost unnoticed past the fussy censor of the thinking mind, which lacks the ability to handle such a 'simple complexity.' Sometimes the meaning registers at the time; at other times the cumulative effect is all that registers.

Dining hall (MG)

At one time, I became embarrassed at having to leave some of the large portions of food put out. Somebody noticed this, and like magic the next day, an extra-plate appeared from nowhere, so that I could leave the excess aside. Somehow, every day after that, on that visit, the extra plate was there, at the right place on the table. Another day, when there were beans, one of the monks checked to learn whether I could eat them safely. Apparently a few people have bad trouble with what they call *'gigantes'* – the enormous broad-beans common in Greece. If I was such a person, they would get me some *'macaronia.'*

Finally, on my last full day, a fast day, when I was having some trouble with digestion, Father A found some sweetened milk that greatly helped. On my last morning, breakfasting in the garden cottage, there was milk for all, a tactful and considerate solution if ever there was one. Otherwise, they left me free to join in their asceticism.

Preparing Vegetables

It was then the custom at Gregoriou for everyone – including guests – to sit together before or after supper to prepare the vegetables brought in from the fields. One day, it was almonds to shell. Another, it was artichokes to be prepared, then spinach; twice it was the everlasting *gigantes* beans. Some twenty or more monks and guests would gather, and the work was done quickly and efficiently. Sometimes the monks would make jokes. Short conversations arose, but by consent, not by outside control, were never allowed to spread into general chatter. If it went too far, one of the monks would begin to repeat the Jesus prayer out loud.

Sometimes they would sing, and often what they sang, always a happy song, would be one of the hymns from recent services, something that said a lot for the unity of their life. Another thing was the way they sometimes conveyed things by kind and gentle object lessons, and, once they were convinced of my sincerity, simply by opening previously closed doors and providing opportunities for me to see what was going on. For example, I was invited into the narthex of the church, normally closed to non-Orthodox.

The Abbot arranged on another occasion that I should sit on a specially placed chair right by the door into the nave, so that I could see the whole liturgy and get a very real feeling of the worship. Many of the main meals were an elaborate ceremonial, begun with procession and prayers.

During one of these meals, just once, occurred another piece of non-verbal teaching. Simply, in an obvious reflection on a well-known Gospel passage, one guest was led by one of the monks to the head of the guest table, and other guests asked to make room for him.

Mysterion

"But we speak the wisdom of God in a mystery, even the hidden wisdom which God ordained before the world unto our glory." (I Corinthians 2, 7)

147

"Behold, I show you a mystery; We shall not all sleep, but we shall all be changed." (Corinthians 15, 51)

"Sacrament, what is sacrament?" asked Father A, during one of our later conversations. We were talking in the unlit guest house reception room, in the blue dusk after Compline looking out from on-high over the still and empty sea. Out of the main line of view, off the headland, the bright lamps of three night-fishing boats lay close together in the shadow under the cliffs that hid the monastery of Simonas Petra. In answer to his question, I mentioned liturgy, confession, baptism. *"Oh,"* he said, *"you mean the mysteries."*

On Mount Athos, one word whose original meaning is remembered is *mysterion*. The Greek roots of this word, going back thousands of years, refer to *'closed mouth and eyes.'* Mysteries are not to be seen with the senses, nor spoken nor written about in any but the most indirect way. *"I shall not speak of Thy mystery to Thine enemies,"* says the Orthodox liturgy. In this, *mysterion* refers primarily to the Eucharist. It seems clear too that, originally, the word 'mystery' had in Christianity something of the same meaning it seems to have had in pre-Christian Greece – speaking of something that could not be observed directly, because it could be known to most of us only by the changes it made in other men and women.

And here on the Holy Mountain, I have reason to believe, the 'mysteries' of the Early Church are remembered, preserved, made-accessible to those who will put themselves out of the way. This, of course is one aspect of 'death,' which Father A described as part of a monk's life, and he also spoke of a briefer 'death of self' that sometimes occurs to the pilgrim visiting Athos.

THE MYSTERY IN MAN

It is of course wrong to associate mystery with any physical location. Even on Athos, the mystery itself is perhaps no more physically accessible than in our Western world, but special conditions exist both in the monastic environment, and in the predispositions of almost two-thousand monks at the same time, most of whom have turned towards the mystery day after day, year after year, century after century, so that this human element makes it more accessible. (More correctly, perhaps, it is the conditions there which make us more open to the mystery?)

Certainly, even in Britain, the same mystery is known to some intellectually, and to a few in more than a merely intellectual way.

But as a culture, we have forgotten or no longer believe in the very idea of a mystery that our modern ways of thought are unable to explain. Certainly, we are unable to accept the ancient idea that something can be true, yet may not be directly and simply explained.

Tautologically, of course, words cannot say much about the inexplicable. Because of this fact, little can be gained by repeating conversations with many different monks, all of which have contained the same basic fact, the idea that mystery and sacrament are beyond language. About these things, one often discovers that one can speak only about what they are not. This is the underlying principle behind what is called *apophatic* theology. The reason for all this became much clearer on one of my Spring visits.

ABSENCE OF THE ABBOT

On Athos, things anyway move in a mysterious way. On the next visit, I found that both the Abbott and Father S were absent. This could have been a great disappointment, as the *geron,* unseen, had so clearly inspired many of my previous experiences at the monastery. But a 'non-Atomist' Athos somehow is not so dependent on even the best of individuals.

My friend Father A had, on this later visit of mine, two main roles in the monastery: he was responsible for the *typikon* that decides what shall be said or sung, controlling the minute-to-minute organization of the services, and he was also baker of the dedicated bread – the *'prosphora'* loaves, used in the Eucharist, a role he performed during the liturgy in a special bakery, with a stone-oven heated by a bright wood-fire. Thanks to both of these things, and to the help of my many other friends among the monks, the visit revealed to me something more of the underlying and essentially Christian 'Athos experience.' It was then that events began which led to the service in the small chapel to which I referred to earlier.

149

CHAPTER 13

4TH VISIT

Katholikon interior (MG)

Always, since I began to visit the monastery, there had been a minor mystery. I would go into the church at the beginning of *Orthros* (Matins). The puzzling event occurred on most days, at the end of Matins, but before the Liturgy proper, when there would be a general movement around and from the church.

Often, at the end of this, very few monks would remain in the big church for the main service of the day. Clearly, one or two were needed in the kitchens. I had never understood where the rest disappeared to. On my fourth visit to Athos, I began to discover some answers. To begin, I spent one morning in the old bakery, where Father A baked the *prosphora* bread used in the communion service.

The monastery has in fact two bakeries: one is quite large, and lies below the inner courtyard of the monastery. Here, a great over-full of bread for the monastery is baked whenever needed.

The other bakery was an ancient building in the oldest part of the monastery, next to the ruins of the defensive tower that once dominated the landward side of the whole complex.

On the concrete floor of this small, gloomy space was a small baker's oven, tables, a few old chairs, all that is needed to bake *prosphora* once a week for the monastery, as well as for a number of smaller communities that had no bakers' oven.

This baking is regarded as part of the Liturgy, understood as proceeding throughout the monastery, not only in the main church, so that the baking and other morning tasks were included in the service.

On this morning, I was standing in the Katholikon at the end of Matins when Father A came up to me and beckoned. I followed him back out of the still-dark church, with its tiny flickering candle-flames and dancing shadows, and its hunched black figures praying in the stalls around the sides.

We went out, up the side of the church, up a long shadowed flight of concrete steps and so, treading with care in the first faint light before dawn, we came up into the bakehouse, a sudden shock of heat in the cool of the early morning, with a gas-lamp hissing in the ceiling, a roaring wood fire under the oven, and the door closed to keep up the temperature so that the blanket-covered dough would rise.

The work was already proceeding at the hands of a young monk, robes in disarray. He was assisted by a novice, a then and always smiling, French-speaking African from the monastery's mission in Zaire. He had come to Gregoriou to learn Greek, and to learn to chant – and later to teach – the complex Byzantine music of the monastic services.

All three monks were sweating profusely as they worked in the heat from the furnace. They were busy cutting-off more dough, rolling it into double balls, and pressing these flat with carved wooden seals that stamp into every small loaf, in Greek, the two thousand year old Gospel message that *'Jesus Christ conquers,'* itself a mystery.

151

I remembered how, at my first Athos Easter the year before, the Abbott, considerate, had permitted me to enter the *litei*, the second room of the four-room Athonite Katholikon, which is normally open only to the Orthodox. Later, he had allowed me briefly into the Katholikon, (the name for the main 'nave' of an Orthodox church,) on Easter Sunday, when, like the monks, I received a candle from his hands to hold for the great Paschal Liturgy.

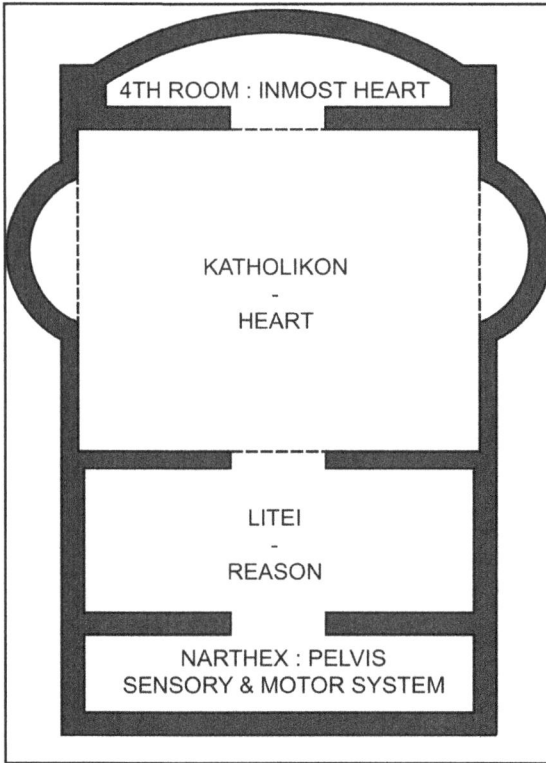

4TH ROOM : INMOST HEART

KATHOLIKON
-
HEART

LITEI
-
REASON

NARTHEX : PELVIS
SENSORY & MOTOR SYSTEM

Floor plan of Katholikon

MEANING OF SORROW

Finally, during one service celebrating the Mother of God as Giver of Life, he had a chair placed for me near the doorway into the nave, so that I could get an even better view of the service. Here, I began to sense things new and strange to me: among them all, perhaps the most significant was the fact that a great stillness would come over me at the same point in each service.

However, at the beginning I did not know enough Greek or enough about the service to recognize even that it was the same point. On at least one occasion, too, I sensed some gift of strength as the *geron* censed me.

Negative theology is theology that approaches God in terms of what He is not. On the next day and after it, the quality of this period of silence during the Liturgy changed for me. As it began, I would find a great sorrow welling up, for what reason I did not know.

"At the moment of the epiklesis," says Abbot Vasileios, *"our offering to God, 'in all and for all,' brings grace to us, being in itself our entreaty, prayer and supplication to the Father to send down the Holy Spirit."* (Archimandrite Vasileios, Abbot of Stavronikita: *Hymn of Entry*)

The love I now felt for the Holy Mountain, and for the monks that had befriended me there, would merge with this mysterious alchemical sorrow. Tears emerged from the stillness of my heart for no good external reason, so that I began to understand – or at least obtain a first sense of – the mystery in which sorrow and joy lie close together.

MICHAEL MUSTAKOV

In some strange way, the whole visit reflected something entirely different said to me by an aristocratic Bulgarian gentleman whose ancestors, centuries ago in Byzantine times, had helped to endow the Bulgarian monastery of Zographou, on the Northern part of Athos. He, like myself, was a regular visitor to Athos. We were talking during dinner in one of the beach cafes of Ouranoupolis, just after his return from Zographou. He was part of that environment where the answers are sometimes bigger than our questions.

"On Athos are many surprising things, but to see them you must be awake," he said. *"This being awake is something known by us Eastern peoples, but I think you know what I mean?"*

When I tried to question him about this later, he denied any memory of having said it. On another occasion, I was talking to the *Hegumenos* of a small community about the early fathers' concept of the *'heart,'* a concept which is very different from our modern

153

Western concept. *"Ah,"* he said to me, *"to waken the heart, that is the thing, yes, that is the thing. But difficult."*

During nearly thirty years of a search for 'truth,' I have several times, as I like to put it, 'fallen through a hole' in my beliefs. These 'magic moments' were times when I had found myself unexpectedly 'woken' to something deeper and more subtle than that with which I began. Now again, as I entered Mount Athos, this kind of change occurred.

This time I fell through into a new and broader idea of the early Christian concept of the heart – a concept that exists in both Christian and Eastern thought. This time, one difference was that I was to some extent aware of the change as it was occurring. The now familiar emergence of the tears which the early fathers called *katanyxis* – compunction – was the beginning of such a breakthrough, my first introduction to this mystery as it emerges on Athos, an aspect of the mystery that, to put it simplistically, silences-thought, and so wakens the sleeping heart. Jesus talks about suffering as the gateway to this perception: *"If you had known how to suffer, you would have been able not to suffer. Learn how to suffer, and you shall be able not to suffer."* *(Gospel of St. Thomas, the Acts of John)* A year later, I had become Orthodox, yet still I find that mystery closer to me on Athos than anywhere else on earth.

After a short while, the younger monk and the novice left the bakehouse, their work done, to join a liturgy in one of the smaller chapels. Three of us still sat there waiting. At such a time, after the long hours of Matins before the dawn, there was emotion in the simple facts of baking; stillness as the rows of tiny loaves stood on the table, soon to be slid into the hot oven; peace as I sat drinking a cup of cocoa, a kindness because Father A knew that my stomach had trouble with monastery food.

Occasionally, something would be explained to me: the reason and symbolic meaning of the seal on the little loaves, so often described in books, but without the same relevance to what was happening. Here, its immediacy gave it so much more meaning; the very fact that this baking was part of the liturgy, because the one liturgy went on throughout the monastery, taking different forms in different places.

For the bread had to be ready for the midday boat that carried some of the tiny loaves, still-warm from the oven, to the hermitages of Karoulia, out at the tip of Athos. Finally, the first loaves were removed, and a new batch took their place in the long, narrow stone oven.

"Try it," said Father A, passing me a loaf from the first batch. Afterwards he gave me a tiny loaf to take away for myself, with another to take back to my wife ... *"A taste of Athos for her!"*

Thus, it was towards the end of the bake, as the plastic bags of *prosphora* were being labeled to be sent off in the boat to the rocky 'desert' at Athos' tip, when I finally rejoined the monks celebrating the Liturgy in the Katholikon, already in bright daylight, with the windows open to the fresh air. But now I had gained something else as well. When I had come to the Holy Mountain on this visit, I had experienced my usual difficulties: yet now they had been replaced by a well of stillness. Often tasted before, this inner peace remained with me throughout my visit ... a 'taste of Athos' indeed.

It was within this stillness that my next glimpses of mystery arose. My request to be able to take confession had been answered. Because of the language problem, Father A would translate and Father P officiate. During the day, a group of six choirboys had arrived from the monastic school at Karyes. They had intended to visit Simonos Petra, but because that monastery was overfull, would stay in Gregoriou overnight ... a fact whose significance will soon become apparent.

After Vespers, I went that evening with Father A and the priest, Father P, to one of the two small chapels, one above the other, in the guest house. There, in the atmosphere of the confessional, and with these two monks I had learned to trust, I raised the problem that was my main concern at the time: impatience. Over busy, tightly-sched-uled years, I had grown increasingly impatient with delays and dis-tractions. In England I had found myself disturbed by the activities of the ever-present small children in Sunday services, and I did not much approve of the 'me' that resulted from this. I asked the Lord's mercy to free me from this burden of the past. Later, in my room, some time after confession, and as I was settling down to sleep, a deeper-than-ever peace came over me.

155

Something happened, but I cannot say what it was. An unseen hand brushed me, and although I was aware of it, even its effects are difficult to catalogue.

The next day, Matins at 3 am found me in the church, where I was directed by Father A, who was again the *'typikon,'* the monk responsible for organizing the sequence of the service. He led me to a seat in the semi-circular choir stalls. There, I found myself seated – by accident or intent – among the fidgeting choirboys ... but experiencing little disturbance. Something had happened to me that I could never hope to explain.

A demon had been cast-out, and who can say whether it was symbolic or real. All I can say is, it had no sensible substance, yet demonstrated considerable power ... so that it is easy to believe that *"this kind can be cast out only by prayer and fasting."* (Mark 9:29)

After that I was – for a while – considerably less impatient. Ask a psychiatrist which is more real, a theory or a compulsion? Something had bidden a compulsion depart ... and it had lost much of its power.

CEMETERY CHAPEL LITURGY

The next morning, after the three-hour Matins, I was taken again up the steps, this time past the small bakehouse and through a small gate in the monastery wall. We crept in the dawn light down a short path to a domed stone chapel looking out to the sea. Here, in the superbly frescoed cemetery-chapel, today's Liturgy would be held. Present for part or all of the service were a number of familiar monks. I was guided to a seat, and the service began. I wondered whether my memory was playing me tricks.

This related directly to the Byzantine tones used by the monks, whose chanting makes great use of prolonged drone-notes. The architecture of the cemetery chapel seemed to me particularly to amplify or augment the most fundamental of all these drone notes, a tone which – as I had discovered in the past – tends to induce or enhance peace of mind. Once again, in the results of their work was the intriguing hint that someone there knows or had known more than they were telling.

Later, I was shown that there were echo-chambers in the ceiling and walls. Yet this was of little importance compared to the real but indescribable significance of my first communion on Athos.

Some hours later in the day, I was sitting beside the big pine tree overlooking the jetty, trying to sort out the many and fast-changing impressions of my visit. I would alternate between periods of questioning, and periods repeating the Jesus prayer, as the stillness of the water reflected the stillness within. Somewhere, across the little cove, a muleteer shouted at his charges as they began their journey into the forested center of Athos. Birds sang.

The novices practiced their chanting in the music school that occupied the top floor of the old building outside the monastery gate – a balconied-building, built against the cliff, which also housed the carpenter's shop.

Bees shopped lackadaisically at the broom on the cliff below me. A fishing boat moved slowly across the horizon. Behind all these sounds lay the stillness of Athos ... a stillness within me. Within that stillness emerged a presence I can never describe. I was not then even sure how to put a name to the presence. I am still not sure. But Abbot Vasileios again has words for the indescribable, for the event, as well as for that which gave it life: *"Thus the statement 'For Thou art God ineffable, incomprehensible, invisible, inconceivable ...' rises before us like a very mountain, steep and hard to approach, from Which the uncreated breeze descends and swells the lungs of man, bringing life to his innermost parts with the joy of freedom, of something unqualified, dangerous, and wholly alive. How often we want to make God conceivable, expressible, visible, perceptible to worldly senses. How much we want to worship idols ... The Divine Liturgy, however, does not allow us to do anything of the sort. It destroys our idols of God, and raises up before us His saving Image, the Word 'who is the image of the invisible God'* (Colossians 1:15), *the archetype of our true, hidden and God-made being."* (Archimandrite Vasileios, Abbot of Stavronikita: *Hymn of Entry)*

In words, nothing had changed. Yet in my heart, something had happened again. Something had touched me, and had left a memory of its passing ... 'a memory with no image,' which closed the eyes of the mind, gently upset my preconceptions, destroyed all my idols,

157

and took my idea of Christ and Christianity beyond the modern ideas that 'he must have been a great teacher,' and that Christianity is a great teaching, to something greater still.

"God," said Evagrius of Pontus, *"cannot be grasped by the mind. If He could be grasped, He would not be God."* (Evagrius, quoted in *'The Orthodox Way,'* by Kallistos Ware)

Truly, I had 'fallen through the hole' once again, had discovered another 'reality' behind the 'reality' I had discovered before. In the Garden of *Panagia,* a seed had begun to grow.

FR. S IN HIS CELL

I first began to glimpse what that seed might grow into on that same visit. My friend, the monk Father S, who was by then in his sixties, was ill. They were not expecting him to live long, and the loss of this simple and kindly old monk with his many years of experience would be greatly felt by the monastery. I asked if I might see him where he lay, and, on this occasion, was allowed into the cell.

He lay there in great simplicity, in a cell that had never – in several centuries – been 're-plastered' as it would be in the West. A few small icons hung on the wall. On nails at one end were the leathers and ropes and simple tools of his profession: he was the monk who cared for the monastery's trees. But most noticeable was his face. Although drawn by illness, it was not only serene, but happy. I asked him how he was. The reply was translated by Father P. *"He is happy. It is a pity to go now, but cannot be avoided, his body was damaged during the war with the Germans – damaged by lack of food. But he says it is nothing to worry about. His time is probably up."* He paused, translated a query about my health and that of our autistic son Nicholas.

He then passed on a query from Father S. A French doctor had suggested some medicine that had been unobtainable in Greece. Could I find it in England? I promised to try.

Finally, after a little more translated conversation, we clasped hands, and I left to allow the sick monk to sleep ... little knowing that when I returned in six months he would be up and around again, and once again making his weak jokes that were so difficult to translate. Before that return, I had managed to obtain the medicine requested, but I doubt that it was that which caused the recovery. The monks on Athos have another medicine, whose strength I have only just begun to learn.

Monastery Gregoriou Katholikon (RA)

CHAPTER 14

THOUSAND-YEAR CLOCK

"The greatest harm done by our own inner impulses is to make us forget that we are the children of a King." (Hasidic teacher)

The strangest thing about Athos is how this complex Christianity of the Church formed by the Early Fathers stayed relatively unchanged in the deep freeze of history, first surviving the breakup of the Byzantine Empire, and its premature extinction; then remaining intact through the motley triumphs and ragged tragedies of the Middle Ages; and finally, or perhaps even now not finally, first through the liberation of Greece from the Turks, and finally surviving the greater triumph, the more disastrous wars, and perhaps greater tragedy, of the spread of what we today call Western Civilization.

The more I learn of Athos, the more I myself believe that the Holy Mountain of today really does contain reflections of the kind of *self-knowledge* which was known on Athos almost 2000 years ago; that by visiting some parts of Athos, you almost literally visit a saner, more-Christian past. I also believe that the secret of the durability of Athos as a society is due not only to its terrain, but to certain quite specific factors, of which this remarkable terrain is only a part. So this Garden of *Panagia* is aptly named. It has clearly been tilled by a master gardener – or gardeners – whose plan brings forth, at the very least, *'fruits unto repentance'* (Luke 3:8) ... a garden which, by its nature, brings-together men of real holiness, generation after generation, and by doing so, maintains its own spirit in such a way that its outward character remains little changed over the years.

Athos contains a unique school for boys. But the true monastic 'schools' are not for children. They teach a view of Christian repentance which is today unique – and uniquely effective. The demands they find on Athos change many men, while leaving Athos itself little-changed. In a continually changing world, such stability is little short of miraculous.

Remarkably, my observations suggest that the survival of Athos and its difficulties actually depends on those difficulties, and on the effects those difficulties create. As long as these difficulties remain, they will make the same demands on both monk and pilgrim, and the special demands they make of them will help to make a special kind of men. My experience of Athos has suggested – forcibly if uncomfortably to me – that it is these frictions that produce self-knowledge, that this self-knowledge is the foundation of stability, and that as long as those demands remain to challenge monk and pilgrim, Athos will continue to produce changed-men.

This friction acts in particular when its effects are emotional. But this is only true of those who do not create for themselves mental sedatives. For those who can avoid this contemporary habit-of-mind, this self-calming – obtaining self-knowledge for themselves becomes a cause of repentance – and so of waking the heart. Here, a romantic streak suggests, is the supposedly mythical 'perpetual motion' machine sought by the sages of the Middle Ages. It has a mountain for its frame, men for its gears, and the Divine Liturgy as mainspring of this *'thousand year clock,'* a clock of which some would say that it continues to run not because of its lack of friction, but because it creates friction in the right ways and the right places.

My clearest demonstration of the realities which lie behind this fanciful description occurred on my second attempt to visit the hermit Father Paisios. As difficult as my first visit, this journey seemed at first a great disappointment, but I later realized that it had simply taught me about ways of learning that did not depend purely on verbal instruction.

2ND VISIT TO FATHER PAISIOS

Between these two visits, there had been a visit to Athos when I had not called on the hermit, believing – perhaps correctly - that his time was too important to waste unless I had a definite reason for seeing him. On this later visit, I had talked to a young Canadian who had been much helped by the hermit, and who was, when we talked, just beginning his trial-period as a monk in Simonos Petra.

Hermitage of Fr. Paisios (RA)

When I first met him, he had been talkative and overactive. Later, when I saw him in the Katholicon of Simonos Petra, he was so different that I barely recognized him. During the service, he was totally still and recollected. Unaware of the depth of the change in him, I tried to greet him discreetly, and was totally ignored. At first I found this strange, but later, I saw that there was good reason for it. At other times, indeed, he was as open and friendly as ever. He was just infinitely more still than he had been in the past. In conversation, it was clear that he thought very highly of Father Paisios, yet he would say little about him. What he did say particularly emphasized the difficulty of seeing this remarkable hermit. Many people, said my friend, tried to see him without success. He spent time in prayer, and would not interrupt his prayer for callers. And there were so many visitors.

Later still, when I left Gregoriou to attempt to see Father Paisios for the second time on my way back to 'Civilization,' I talked briefly about him with the monk I described as Father P, who lived at Gregoriou. I was standing by the jetty waiting for the caique to Dafni, and had mentioned that I hoped to see the hermit enroute.

I would be permitted to stay the following night in the Gregoriou Konachi, the monastery's residence in Karyes, (where each of the twenty ruling monasteries of Athos has a residence for its council representatives). The warmth of the monk as he spoke of the hermit was clearly visible.

"He's a saint, a real saint," he told me, expressing a fact that is now fully recognized. His face softened, and his eyes filled with tears at the thought. *"A real holy-man. We are very lucky he is here with us."* Father P paused a moment and looked up at me. *"He is also a very busy man. Often when people go there, he does not see them. If so, you must not be disappointed."*

Just then, the *caique* appeared around the rocky point below the monastery, and we busied ourselves saying goodbye.

PEIRASMOS OF PILGRIMAGE

Much is hidden in the Greek word *peirasmos:* test, or temptation. Life is *peirasmos.* The difficulties that emerge on pilgrimage are an intensification of this testing or temptation. The intensification arises in part because the pilgrim has stood out from all the modern aids and comforts we are accustomed to in the West. In practice, this means that the *peirasmos*, the tests and frictions of life, are not so easily avoided by the pilgrim. Perhaps a pilgrim should not even try to avoid them ... for by avoiding them it seems as if we avoid a part of ourselves. If it is true that freedom – and salvation too – are only for those who are whole, then *peirasmos* tests that wholeness and shows us where it is not yet complete.

Many years ago I was told that I did not understand the use of questions: questions are not only to obtain answers, they also serve, even if unanswered, to direct someone's attention, normally to things they ignore or have forgotten.

Peirasmos describes a similar process, in which unexpected events test us by drawing to the surface aspects, often weaknesses, in our nature, and often – it seems to me – do so in conditions where we will notice these flaws.

Often what emerges are old habits which seem harmless under normal conditions, yet whose harmful nature is clearly visible in the different conditions of those 'tests' that repeatedly occur on Athos. It is then that one begins to see the need to give up some habit. This is what it means that testing is a means to self-knowledge. God tests us because we need to know ourselves. Or we may place ourselves in testing conditions, perhaps by submitting to the frictions of pilgrimage in order to know ourselves better.

In modern life, we barely notice the temptations to which we are exposed, for they have become too universal. We learn to live with them, enjoy them, exploit them in others. To understand how temptations can become so commonplace that we do not really notice them, we need to be placed in a position where they become clearly visible. Athos as a whole is such a place. There, one more easily sees oneself being tempted ... or observes that one had just unconsciously succumbed to temptation. In this view, this later visit to Father Paisios was a perfect example of *peirasmos* in its main sense of temptation.

On the trip from Gregoriou, I had been thinking about the hermit's instruction, given to me a year ago, to think about the good things done by others. As I thought about it, I realized that I had too rarely carried out this instruction. Yet now, a year later, I kept noticing my own weaknesses. For instance when the usual crowd of teenagers rushed to the door of the bus at Dafni, I became quite upset and began to work my way to the front of the queue. Afterward, looking back from the relative comfort of my seat, I felt a strange discomfort that I should behave in such a way, particularly in this place.

From this beginning, the whole visit began to become more and more like one of the ancient myths. I kept on acting in ways that I regretted. And the closer I got to Father Paisios, the more aware I became of my own little selfishnesses.

Again, on this visit, I was unable to find an interpreter. First, the monks were too busy for anyone to spare the time to come with me. Then, right into the afternoon in Karyes I failed to find anyone.

But I remembered how St. Anthony the Great is said to have had three regular visitors. Two were always asking questions, the third was always silent. Asked by the saint why he had no questions, this monk said: *"For me it is enough to see you."*

Encouraged by this story, I decided to try to see Father Paisios anyway, with or without interpreter. I told the monks where I was going, and set off alone through the forest to the hermit's cell.

THE HERMIT'S CELL

Later, I crossed the little stream, and walked between tall chestnut trees until I saw the high fence that surrounded Father Paisios's cell. Sitting by the gate on upended logs were three of the teenagers who had been so pushy when getting on the bus. Now they were friendly. Obviously they, like me, had simply been worried about finding space on the bus.

Today, they had rung Father Paisios's ingenious bell a few times, but nobody had responded. They tried again as I watched. Again no response. We waited. I wrote a brief note in English in the hope that the Father might be able to get it translated, and put it with others in the jam jar left for the purpose. High in the trees, an occasional bird sang. In the distance I heard mule-bells. The sound of a lorry grumbled up a hill, faded, emerged again, and rumbled away into the distance. Up the hill, a twig snapped. Voices talked, barely audible. We sat, occasionally fidgeting from the discomfort, or seeking better shade. The young men talked together. Eventually two got up and left, leaving one who spoke a little English. I tugged at the bell again ... and again some ten minutes later.

Still nothing happened.

An old monk appeared with a tall and troubled looking young man, looked at the gate, and walked on around the fence. A few minutes later, two middle aged men appeared in blue T-shirts. I had seen them too on the bus. One of them walked up to the bell and tugged it. Again, it tinkled softly among the trees. Again, nothing happened for a moment, then there was a call from the balcony of the *kelli*. The hermit had finished his prayers. After a brief conversation, the key arrived, and the gate was opened.

The hermit shouted some instruction. *"One group at a time,"* the young man interpreted for me.

The two latest arrivals began walking up the path to the cell. Habitually, I began to remonstrate, realized rather too late how inappropriate it was in this situation, and stopped. Too late! The old man called out again: *"All come, then."*

With a rather red face, I followed the others up the path, feeling a sorrow because I had brought my Western-ways with me. On the short climb up the well worn path, I saw much of myself, and I did not particularly like what I saw. Seeing the foolishness of one's habitual behavior in this way not only helps us know ourselves, it certainly generates compunction, and that compunction as clearly makes us more conscious, and so for a while more able to make right decisions. So it was that, in the sunlight in front of the cell, I joined an odd assortment of human beings; Greek youths with hiking gear, two middle-aged Greek men in traveling clothes, myself, English with a middle-age spread.

The old hermit, true to his calling, fetched mugs of crystal clear water, passed around the traditional loukoumi, and began asking what people wanted from him. He recognized me, and asked through the young man: *"Are you the Englishman who was here last year?"*

I nodded. He smiled and squeezed my arm in greeting. He took my temporary interpreter on one side and spoke for a few minutes, then left us to let the last two arrivals explain the purpose of their visit.

Now, from the nearer fence at the rear of the little cottage came a shout in Greek. There was another gate there, hidden among a thick stand of laurel. There was the leathery old monk with his young protégé. The hermit quickly broke off his conversation, and went immediately to unlock the back gate and let the new visitors into the compound. He returned very briefly to his conversation ... and a minute later, the two men were off down the path to the lower gate. Father Paisios said something in Greek.

"Go now", said the young man in English. I did not take it in for a moment. Buffered by my lack of Greek, I at first decided he hadn't been speaking to me.

166

My translator was told a last few words by the hermit before he left. *"Must go now,"* he repeated. I looked around. The hermit was already deep in conversation with the old monk. The young man with him looked more than ever troubled.

Clearly, I must leave right now.

LEARNING WITHOUT WORDS

It was several hours before the realization broke upon me that I had learned as much on this visit as on my previous visit, when I had spent much time in conversation with the old man. Almost wordlessly, I had learned something about myself. I had also learned something about Athos; perhaps even about the mechanisms by which the Holy Mountain has so successfully maintained its purposes for a thousand years. I had even learned – and this was even more valuable – a little about how to learn about myself.

As we went out through the gate of the compound, hooking the big padlock back into position, the young man asked me: *"Karyes?"* I nodded. *"I go Ivirion,"* he continued. *"Good luck on your visit."*

I thanked him, wished him a good visit, and began my walk back to the konachi. After an early night and an early service, with a wind strong in the big chestnut-trees behind the low stone konachi, I walked along dew-wet paths to the center of Karyes, where I joined the mob of monks and pilgrims waiting for the bus to Dafni.

The time came for the bus to set-out. Nothing happened. Then a ripple of agitation and uncertainty. People began to wander around looking for information. Niko, son of our landlady in Ouranoupolis, then on Athos doing some engineering work for one of the monasteries, was waiting for the same bus. He came up to me. *"No boat today, Mr. Amis, so the bus is not running."* He paused. *"I have to get back today. Business."* It was the first time I had heard the word 'business' on Athos. Niko shook my hand and disappeared. By now, the square was empty of monks. All who remained were unaccompanied pilgrims, most of them by now looking puzzled. I began to look forward with some semblance of horror to another night in the nearby hotel, then the familiar figure of Father A came round the corner into the square, beckoning to me.

167

"No boat, no bus," he said in French. He smiled.

"Konachi," he said, *"Bienvenue."* I walked with him to the Gregoriou *konachi* in the woods outside Karyes.

WALKING TO XEROPOTAMOU

Signs marking the paths (MG)

Other things, too, have made it clear to me that on Athos it is not so much what you think or say that matters, as what you are. This is why it makes most sense next to talk about another journey altogether, by writing about my first visit to the ancient monastery of Xeropotamou, ('dry river'), which lay beside the road back down to Dafni. On this occasion, I had returned to the square at Karyes, after a morning visit to Father Paisios, only to discover that the bus to Dafni had already left, I think somewhat-earlier than announced. Rashly, as my legs were giving me some trouble, I decided to walk to Xeropotamou, and go on to Dafni the next day. So I organized my baggage for carrying, and studied the map.

The bus passes Xeropotamou, but its route from Karyes goes up a long and sandy road, which first heads away from the West-Coast of Athos, and only gradually turns about and, crossing the great central ridge, begins the long run downhill to the sea.

168

A shorter but very much steeper mule-track runs from the other end of Karyes, zigzagging up the slopes of the high forested-ridge behind the town, until it meets the motor road at the crest, hundreds of feet above the highest towers of the town. It took me two hours to climb this track, mostly in shade.

Much of this way, I walked with a kind American scholar whose summer researches involved cataloging the never-before publicly-listed monastery libraries. I rather slowed him down, because – I think – he believed the hill might be too much for me. Thank you, kind scholar.

Finally reaching the top of the ridge, another two hours took me down a much longer open road to the sea, stopping for every usable patch of shade. Eventually, after walking down a long stone-block mule track, where all the shade trees had been felled to clear a path for telephone lines, and then passing round the last of a series of hairpin bends in the descending road high above the sea, I reached the drinking fountain by the monastery gate, where I gratefully took a drink of cool water in the shade of a clump of olive trees. After a few minutes, feeling stronger, I looked around for the entrance to the monastery, but could not find it. Is this too a parable, an icon: a fountain made ready for the traveler, but the gate hidden? Probably the symbolism was not intentional: the building of a wide new road, completed only the year or so before, has left the monastery's main-gate rather inaccessible and increased the traffic to its tiny back door which was concealed in a corner of the ancient stone buildings.

Entering this small doorway, I emerged on concrete staging at about first floor level, with arches giving a view of the monastery's big courtyard. There was nobody around, just a framed plan of the monastery on one wall. Helpfully, this showed another exit, as well as the location of the guest house. I had to go down one staircase, across the courtyard, and up a high flight of steps in the opposite side of the monastery square. Once inside, there were two more stories to climb, a slow task after my two walks, one to see Father Paisios, then this second to Xeropotamou. Finally, I reached the reception area of the guest house and rang the brass bell.

A few minutes later, a young monk arrived with his arm full of bedlinen, put it in a room to one side, and came back with the regulation raki, water, and loukoumi. Did I want a bed for the night? I said please, if it was possible, not knowing how I would otherwise reach any other haven on rubber-legs that had walked more that day than in the previous month.

He gestured to the visitor's book. I filled in the columns: name, passport number, *diamonitirion* number, occupation. He left me to finish my drink, then came back and showed me to a room on the floor below. I toweled-off, changed my shirt, and settled down for a belated siesta.

After little more than an hour, the bell rang for Vespers. I made my way across the wide courtyard, past the cupolaed fountain, in through a side-door to a covered cloister with big glazed windows, and so into the rear of the largest church I had yet found on Athos. There, staying by the back wall, I made my way slowly to one of the carved stalls. As I did so, I passed a tall, hook-nosed old monk, whose white-hair and beard made him look in his seventies. He said in Greek some words I could not recognize, but I guessed their import. *"Orthodoxus,"* I told him, *"Orthodoxus."* He smiled, and waved me into a stall. The service lasted an hour or so. At the end, as the monks began to troop out of the building, the old monk came up to me: *"Germanos?"* He asked. *"Anglos."* I replied.

"You are welcome." He walked off towards the corner of the church, and a minute late I heard whispered voices, something about: *"Orthodoxus Anglicos."* Obviously, I was something of a rare bird in Xeropotamou. Indeed, it seemed they were not easily-convinced. As the service ended, I was guided by a younger monk into the flow of monks and visitors down the glassed-in cloister, and so into the *trapeza,* the abundantly-frescoed monastery refectory. There, the monks sat at different tables near the windows. Guests were directed to other tables. In this monastery, the monks' tables and one guest-table ran in lines from the main-door to the far, bright-windowed wall. Only one table was then occupied, and I was directed to that. I sat and ate lightly of the meal, then waited while everyone finished, and the Abbot and monks completed the meal with prayers. By then, I was glad to return to my room.

I did so, organized my clothes for dressing in the morning darkness, and was reading in the last of the fading daylight when two other travelers were shown into the room.

Next day the bell for the service woke me about three. I had slept my six hours, and was ready for the service. I waited some twenty minutes, dressed, crossed the uncertain paving of the yard, and crept into the back of the dark church just as the chanting began.

Monks were still coming into the church. Tiny flames flickered, and brass chandeliers gleamed in the gloom. The rich golds and reds of two big icons on their marble stands glowed softly. Dark figures came, saluted the icons, and went on. The celebration was typically Athonite, the long vowels of the Byzantine chanting echoing sonorously through the large church as the stages of the service came and went through the hours. By the time the liturgy began, I felt greatly at peace. With the preparation of the communion, the peace intensified. Involuntarily, I lost myself in the mystery, and my eyes filled once again with tears of *katanyxis*.

Almost an hour later, at the end of the service, I mingled with the stream of monks leaving the church, and again found myself in *trapeza*. As I went to my previous table, the young monk who had guided me on the evening before reached out a hand and instead guided me to the other guest table, parallel to those occupied by the monks, where there were a few older Greek pilgrims, a typical piece of Athonite symbolism, similar to an earlier event at Gregoriou, where one pilgrim had been shown to the head of the guest-table.

This time, at the end of the meal, when one of the monks came round with the blessed bread they call the 'lamb,' it was passed for me to take a pinch ... a sure sign of my acceptance. Later, on my way back to the guest house before leaving, when I passed the monk who had guided me to table, he stopped to talk for a moment, smiling. *"Come and visit us again,"* he told me, after inquiring whether I had been comfortable at the monastery.

The monks of Athos often say very little, but at this and other times it has seemed to me that they see a great deal. It is not what you say and hear that matters here, but what you are, and what you do.

CHAPTER 15

Synergia: co-operation

Icon of the Mother of God

"It is easy to be a monk in one's outer self if one wants to be, but no small struggle is required to be a monk in one's inner self." (The Philokalia: The Complete Text)

In everyday life, everything depends on our own efforts and on our co-operation with our fellow man. In the spiritual life, everything depends on our own efforts and on these coming in line with the Grace of God, a situation called *synergia: (*synergy). But before we can achieve *synergia,* we have to realize that this is not the normal state of man, but something more rare, which it is difficult to attain in its fullness. *Synergia* is one of the high points in the Athonite *'science of the heart:'* one of the primary aims of spiritual training, of ascesis.

In those who come to Athonite monasticism as young men, this is sometimes aided by practices such as that known as *'cutting off the will,'* an arduous discipline that can involve much physical labor, and probably can only be applied to people by someone with special training and experience. Some of the Abbots on Athos, I think, have this skill, although I cannot say whether all of them do.

For lay people, who cannot spend much time on Athos, and perhaps for certain types of monk as well, there exist methods of creating the necessary situation for 'educating the emotions,' using the readily available material found in situations and difficulties of everyday life. This too hinges around the question of will and will-fulness.

What has to be cut off is our willfulness, our personal will. This idea tends to sound to Western ears harsh and even 'un-Christian' but this is only due to a misunderstanding. In fact, the willfulness which is challenged by monasticism is not true will. It actually seems to be a hypnagogic loss of our proper will, which has been captivated by our past; by passions, and by outside pressures. Passions are sustained by external stimuli, but this is sometimes difficult to understand. Recognizing that this 'captivity' is a true representation of the facts is a definite step towards spiritual growth, both for monks, and for laymen.

SYNERGIA AS FREEDOM

Between my visits to Athos, my wife and I had visited a convent near our hotel. There, one of the nuns who spoke English spoke to us of a letter by St. Anthony describing three kinds of men who come to Christ. (These were described at the end of Chapter One.) To remind us: The first need no discipline. The second are those who come to the discipline when young, and can take the difficult ways, such as the cutting off of the will. The third are those who have been more influenced by the pressures of life, and particularly of modern life. It was about them that St. Anthony wrote about *thlipsis* in terms that sound harsh today.

But if one really understands, it begins to look different, because synergy is the proper state of the human will. *Synergia is* therefore the only true freedom to which man can aspire. But to understand this, we have to understand first what are the problems. The basic obstacle to *synergia* is *peirasmos* (temptation).

Looking at this in modern terms, it is quite simply that we succumb to temptation whenever we allow one of our faculties to take priority, instead of using all our faculties to the best.

But even this is not as simple as it seems. There exist all kinds of pressures upon us and within us which can tempt us and bind us in this way. A typical example lies in the fact that whatever we are doing, wherever we are, we almost always want to be somewhere else, or doing something else. In binding us, these impulses also divide us, or in another way of looking at it, when we overcome division, the result shows as patience or endurance: *hypomonie.* This is developed by the effort to endure.

St. Peter Damascenos puts it that: *"The Lord said: 'He who endures patiently to the end will be saved.'"* (Matthew 10:22) *Hypomonie* is said to be the consolidation of all the virtues, because without it, none of them can subsist. *"Whoever turns back is 'not fit for the kingdom of heaven.'"* (Luke 9:62) *Indeed, even though someone thinks he is in possession of all the virtues, he is still not fit for the kingdom until he has first endured to the end and (thus) escaped from the snares of the devil, for only thus can he attain it. Even those who have received a foretaste of the kingdom stand in need of hypomonie if they are to gain their final reward in the age to come. Indeed, persistence is needed in every form of learning or knowledge."* (St. Peter Damascenus, in the *Philokalia*)

A question of age comes into this. Where young monks may be able to undergo the special disciplines entailed in the process of cutting off the will, if an older man comes to monasticism later in life, it is often impossible for such a rigorous discipline to be applied. In this situation, or in monasteries where rigorous methods are not known or not applied, the would-be monk, if he would learn the secret ways of *synergia,* first has to face the same kind of prolonged testing-by-circumstances which the layman lives with every day.

For Western man, all this not only involves enduring physical problems, but more important, it involves learning to trust God, instead of trusting one's own mind, one's own conclusions. So the true Christian must learn to live with uncertainty just as the pilgrim or monk has to learn to live with uncertainty. This, living-with-uncertainty, this *hypomonie*, is surely a forgotten key to spirituality in the West today. Yet even among those who practice regularly, there are differences between monk and layman.

Arising out of centuries of Orthodox culture, in his poem, *'The Monk'* Turgenev gives some idea of the difference between the layman and the monk:

"I have known a monk, a hermit, a saint.
He only lived by and for the sweet taste of prayer,
and when drunk (with this), he remained standing
for so long upon the cold marble floor of the church
that his legs were swollen to just below the knees,
and resembled thick pillars. He felt them no longer;
he was just standing, just praying.

"I understand that man. Maybe I even envied him:
but let him, in his own turn, understand me,
and let him not judge me,
I who do not have access to his bliss.

"This man has succeeded in destroying his 'self,'
in canceling out his hated 'I,' yet when I do not pray
it is not pride which prevents me. My own 'I'
seems heavier to bear and more repulsive
than does his 'I' seem to him.

"He has found that which enables him to forget himself,
but 'I,' too, am able to do so,
although perhaps less constantly than he."

TRANSFORMATION OF ATTITUDE

The pilgrim's uncertainties arise because – for a newcomer – Athos is a land of problems. The problems arise because of the monastic way of life. As a result, pilgrimage evokes its own added *thlipsis,* rooted in the need to trust. Not to trust somebody in the flesh, but to trust God, to trust the universe, to trust things as they are. But not for nothing is Athos known for its little miracles. On this mountain little is planned, so that every meeting is a miracle ... some not so small, yet one is never quite sure! To enter Athos for the first time is very much a leap in the dark. On Athos, I, with all my needs and all my weaknesses, found myself powerless in the hands of God.

This links with the classical Greek idea of *becoming,* still so important to the Greek monk today. It helps to explain much of the special quality of Athonite religious practice. Becoming is more important in an inward than an external way. It is in these places where one can more easily re-establish contact with the eternal in oneself; one can become still, and, becoming still, become more one-self; but *becoming* means more than mere inaction. It is dependence on the eternal: eternal-place; eternal-being; eternally-unchanging, when the human mind can rest and become still. It is in that strange stillness that one begins to become still at the center of one's being, and it is there, as I understand it, that one may find Christ.

Here lies truth, and here open the doors of love. Yet this 'place' is perhaps the least known and least-understood of the inner keys to Athonite psychology. Its elusiveness is expressed in the gospel image of the *'strait-gate:'* imaged in the idea of the 'eye of the needle,' something that, even in its ordinary household sense, is something that demands attentiveness; and here it also explains the parable of the *'Talents,'* as mentioned earlier. More than mere physical stillness, more even than silence of mind, it is the inexpressible silence of the heart. It is thus literally beyond-words; *'seen but not described.'*

If one understands this, one understands much else. Find this, and one finds how to put into practice many ideas that otherwise remain mere theory.

Carry out the instructions of the *geron* with sufficient care and persistence, and it is to this 'place' that one comes. There, briefly, one becomes what one is.

I first glimpsed this place in myself on Athos a short time after I arrived at Simonos Petra, accepting that God's will is more like something within us than something to be learned from outside. But to see this is one thing, to live it another, yet it does mean that one can be true at the same time both to God and to oneself, if only we learn to reflect the right, the God-given, as found within us.

SIN AS MISSING THE MARK

The difficulty, as I have so often found, is that we all too often *'miss this mark:'* missing this mark is called in Greek *hamartia*: 'failure.' This is the word translated in English as sin. One aspect of *hamartia* is described in the parable of the talents. It is the failure to express the divine will.

We are 'synergetically' true to the spirit only when individual action is in some way more than individual; when it is more than self-gratification; more than mere survival and success. To be true to the Spirit is thus a Christian resolution of the conflict between free-dom and society, between individuality and the collective, between self and the common good. It provides an alternative not to one or other side of this conflict, but to the conflict itself. Recent research shows, in fact, that the distinction between man and 'other animals' exists in the human willingness to co-operate. Where conflict is avoidable, it seems, all conflicts between-people are a failure to be fully human.

The full breadth of this idea of being true to something God giv-en-within us was made clearer to me in a conversation I had on my sixth visit, when I again visited the hermit and *geron* Father Paisios. As I emerged from my room, I was introduced to a young man in a khaki sweatshirt: Andreas, a Canadian of Greek ancestry, who was staying with the monks at a nearby kelli. *"They are having difficulty speaking with you,"* he told me after we had been introduced.

"They want to offer hospitality, but do not know what you would wish. Would you like a cup of coffee?"

Coffee duly appeared, and we continued our conversation on the veranda, with its magnificent view of the distant peak of Athos itself. Andreas briefly told me how he was visiting the Holy Mountain for the second time, staying some two-months in the summer before returning to Canada and college. He lived in the cells with the monks, and while he was there, like a monk, came under obedience to the *geron* or elder monk who led that small community.

"But did I want to see Father Paisios?" he asked. The best time would be the next morning. He would be happy to translate for me, but would need the permission of the Father of his kelli first. He would telephone later if the *geron* agreed.

We arranged a time in the morning when he would come, and which would hopefully allow me to return to Karyes in time for the bus to Dafni. Later, a telephone call confirmed that the trip was on.

CONSCIENCE

Iconostasis (MG)

The meaning of the word 'sin' seems to have changed over the years. At one time, the word 'sin' did not imply crime, in the sense of a crime against someone else!

178

Understood properly, if a sin is a crime at all, it is a crime against oneself, and therefore against God. Of course, Victorian attitudes to religion have given us a very negative view of the biblical word translated as 'sin.' This word, *hamartia*, in the Greek, originally meant failure.

More than the ideas of Athos, to participate in any real way in the reality of Athos brings one face-to-face with a different world. In that world, one discovers the more relaxed, more forgiving attitude to sin than exists in much of the West today. A different attitude to life begins to surface within you in response, so that one begins to see this different world everywhere around you: in the attitudes and actions of the monks; in the theology of their church; even in the behavior of nearby villagers.

The big difference lies in the difference of the monk's attitude to things like authority and responsibility. Underlying this is a different way of understanding the concept of the 'Will of God,' a difference which is perhaps crucial to the Orthodox view of life.

We tend to view the Will of God almost legalistically, as something we should learn as we learn ordinary instructions from employers and others ... that is, we regard it almost as a communication. The view on Athos is different, and links instead with the idea of the icon, with the idea of man as made in God's image, the image that had been perfectly manifested by Christ.

God's will, according to this view, already exists within us.

Clearly, this links in some way with the Gospel parable of the talents. God's will is within us waiting to be discovered and expressed, it is not something to be imitated or acquired. Thus to fulfill the Will of God is not to go against one's real nature; 'to be true to the Spirit' is to be true both to God and to oneself, something close to the Western idea of finding and expressing one's 'real self.'

This is also closely related to the best meanings of our modern concept of conscience. This is a big thing, and contains overtones of responsibility. Through my experiences on Athos I have come to see this as giving a wholly different view of virtue. This is a view based on observation, but on observation that is obtained only with difficulty.

It is consistent with the idea that if man is the icon, the image of God, there is an innate goodness in the human being that, once uncovered, needs no outward enforcement.

All we have to do is to become what we are: to be ourselves as God made us: to do what we see to be right according to our inherent sense of what is right, and our best abilities. The full breadth of this is that, by being true to something God-given within us, we are true to God, and by being true to God, we are true to ourselves. This was made clearer to me in a conversation with Father Paisios on my sixth visit to Athos.

This visit to the hermit actually began the day before the one of which I was just speaking, when, after making the journey from Ouranoupolis to Karyes, and having obtained my *diamonitiron*, I walked, already tired, to the Gregoriou Konachi.

"Kali spera," said Father T as he answered the bell and invited me in, ushering me through the wide hall with its great log-chest and its glass doors to the chapel. He led me through into the little living room with its icons, its iron stove, its long window, its long wide benches and hard cushions, just as I remembered it.

"Katse! Katheste!" He invited me to sit, and Father V soon appeared with a full plate of delicious soup with artichokes from the *konachi*'s fertile garden. Then, among friends, we settled down to the serious business of trying to communicate. What did I need? Did I want to see Father Paisios, as they had heard I would? I think that was the gist of it. But with language-problems, the communication did not go well. Soon, I was shown to a room to rest. I opened the windows as wide as I could for the air, and lay down gratefully for siesta. I was wakened two hours later by voices in the hall outside.

FATHER PAISIOS

Next morning I woke around six, and quickly made my way to the chapel to join Father V, who was saying Matins on his own. He had just finished when Andreas arrived and began talking high speed Greek to him.

There followed the embarrassment of piled food, of which I could eat little, since my stomach had not yet adapted either to Athos times nor Athos cooking.

Finally, somewhat later than intended, we left, Father V showing us the unmarked trail that cut straight from the *konachi,* through the thickly-overgrown forest, to the Philotheou mule track, from which a path led to the hermit's cell. The journey was very much shorter than if we had gone through Karyes.

When we got to his kelli, Father Paisios was under the veranda, splitting logs.

"Who is it?" he called in Greek. My interpreter told him it was the Englishman who had been to see him twice before. *"Wait!"* came the reply. We waited. The gentle blows of an axe splitting wood merged into the silence of the forest. The big machines that are working in some of the Athos forests grumbled far away in the background without spoiling the stillness. A quarter of an hour passed. *"Should I try again?"* asked my companion. *"No,"* I said, *"He knows we are here. He will come when he is ready."*

Only two or three minutes later the old man emerged from the bushes near the gate and passed us the key. We followed him up the path, round the cottage to the clearing on the far side where, under a tree, were some half-dozen logs upended beside a larger one that served as a table.

The old-man greeted us, filled mugs with crystal-clear water, left the loukoumi open beside them in traditional Athos hospitality, and disappeared into his home, saying that we had arrived so early that he still had chores to finish.

KNOWING THE WILL OF GOD

Ten minutes later he joined us again, and we began to talk. Again, as had happened on my previous visit without an interpreter, I learned more in the way of practical lessons than by his words. In essence, I discovered that although his words even now had immense value, it would have been better if I had come to him better prepared, after my latest visit to the monasteries and not before, when my mind was still full of the world I had so recently left.

I still regret that I did not think clearly enough at this time to follow up what he said as well as I might.

I also regretted very much that I had not yet learned Greek; the limitations of translation cause real problems when dealing with things both subtle and spiritual. Nevertheless, it was a conversation of great value to me and, I suspect, to others living in the West.

"Jesus tells us," I said at the beginning, *"that we should not simply call on God, but should do the will of God. If I wished to carry out this commandment, what should I be doing in my everyday life?"*

I think my young interpreter put this slightly differently, because the old man seemed slightly disappointed that this was all I was asking, and I remembered then that he had expected me to return at some future time and ask him one special question. That question is still unasked. However, he answered my current question very well, and in my eyes very much simplified the whole idea of doing the Will of God.

It seemed to me that Father Paisios did not talk theory. There was a quality in his advice that eliminated the distance and the imprecision that normally comes between us and important ideas. Thus his words seem to directly link to experience.

He showed me quite precisely what was meant by the idea that we should be open to the best impulses that reach us, and also should be *'deaf to the temptations of our own weaknesses, and of people's attempts to force us into different directions in our lives.'*

There seems to be an element of 'conscience' in this: of *'saying what we feel and doing what we say.'* At the same time, it linked with the idea that to do the will of God we should *'be ourselves,'* should learn to express what God had made of us

THE JUST MAN

In this reconciliation of apparent opposites, as in its reconciliation of the ideas of authority and liberty, this kind of guidance helps to free the mind of its confusing dualities. For example, this different view of doing the will of God has a great power to make life simpler.

"What do you now do for a living?" I was next asked.

I told him, and provided additional details he asked for. *"Is the problem one of honesty?"* I was asked.

"It is important to keep to this kind of honesty even though you do not do so well as a result. In this kind of situation, where the Just Man does what is right, what he sees to be right, he may lose at the time, but God makes it up to him. Let me give you an example. A Greek farmer used to visit me. He had four brothers who were lazy and shiftless, but although a simple soul, he himself had cleared and developed a lot of land, and was doing quite well. His brothers saw this and decided to share in his land. He remembered his obligations, and they were able to take the best pieces, the pieces he had developed most fully. Their brother, with the rocky, unproductive land left to him, came to me in great difficulties. I told him it would be alright, that the Lord would make it come out right in the end.

"I next saw him almost ten years later. 'How are you doing?' I asked him. 'Very well,' he replied, 'the land I had contained valuable minerals, and I am now a rich man. What should I do?' I advised him to help those around him who were poor, and he did this, and built a church, and still was rich. I asked him some time later, how were his brothers: he did not know. They had sold their land and gone off to jobs here and there.

"So God sees what is right, and sees when a man follows what he knows to be right, follows his own heart and not those who try to make him change, and in the long run, He makes it come out right. One must persist in doing what is right, as best one knows, and not take the easy-way, not allow people to force us to compromise.

The man who does this is the just man, the dikaios. God looks after him."

This, doing what was right, was being true to the Spirit. It was not just following the rules of social morality, but doing what the individual knows to be right in his inmost heart, even though others would have one act differently from this. Being true to the spirit depends on conscience; success (as an opposite of *hamartia*) lies in the expression of that knowing ... a very special kind of knowing – the simple knowing of the very young child – then linked in spontaneity with simple action.

The you that 'has ethos' is the you that grows by taking responsibility, and the responsibility it must take is to act on its 'own ethos' – and never respond to outside pressures.

As soon as it responds to outside pressures, that is not spirit, but passion – in the classical sense in which passion was derived from the same root as passive.

According to Origen, it is in knowing this that true son-ship lies. The ordinary servant has to be told what to do externally. By contrast, we are told in the Gospel of St. John Ch. 15:15 that: *'The servants of God know what is in the Father's mind.'*

"For what man knoweth the things of a man, save the spirit of man which is in him; even so the things of God knoweth no man, but the spirit of God. Now we have received, not the spirit of the world, but the spirit which is of God; that we might know the things that are freely given to us of God. For who hath known the mind of the Lord, that he may instruct him? But we have the mind of Christ." (I Corinthians 2: 12 and 16)

This, self-expression by doing the will of God, is the ultimate behavioral paradox, combining in itself aspects of human character which modern thought regards as mutually contradictory. In resisting Henry VIII, Thomas More sought to be true to the spirit, not simply to defend doctrine. Blind-faith is the death of truth, and so it is the negation of true faith. The 'mysteries' of the church do not demand blind faith, although it is easy to imagine that they do.

UNLEARNED

To be in the presence of such a man as Father Paisios somehow restores one's mind to its own best-condition, replacing the uncontrolled changes that occur in us. This means that, to be true to the Spirit, we need to reflect something that exists within us, not things we have learned from other people. (Although the actions of the saints may show us the way.) We must reflect the right, the true, the God-given we find within us. The difficulty, as I have so often found, is that we all too often 'miss this mark,' and it is missing this mark that is the failure of *hamartia*. In its original form, *hamartia* contains no overtones of 'Protestant guilt.'

184

In its original sense, any guilt created by outside influences, by social-forces, is itself a form of *hamartia*. One aspect of *hamartia is* described in the parable of the talents.

Hamartia is also well explained by the pattern in certain Persian carpets. If the weaver makes a mistake in the design, the mistake is retained and becomes part of the design, and the work after this must develop from the mistake. We are true to the spirit only when individual action is in some way more than individual; when it is more than self-gratification, more than survival and success.

In that Greece of which Mount Athos is the heart, the whole concept of *prosopon* – person-hood – which some theologians see as opposed to individuality, might be clearer if described in terms of true as opposed to false individuality.

ST. HESYCHIOS

"If a man does not carry out the will and law of God
in his inward parts, that is, in his heart,
he will not be able to carry them out easily
in the outward sphere of the senses."
(St. Hesychios the Priest, in The Philokalia: The Complete Text)

In the Church, this defines a shared responsibility for ensuring that doctrine remains true to experience, so keeping the original quality of the liturgy, of prayer, and of the sacrament. In life, it is everything which is the responsibility of man: justice in all its forms; good-husbandry; caring for the weak; aiding other individuals to be true to the Spirit; leaving a world fit for future-generations; keeping the minds and acts of our civilization free of harmful ideas.

All such responsibility is important for the contribution it makes to the growth of those who take responsibility. This responsibility of every Christian for the continued truth of Christianity is important in its implications – in just this way. It is through accepting this personal-responsibility for truth that individuals grow more able to perceive truth, so that the very need to protect such a Tradition becomes a force for spiritual growth.

CHAPTER 16

ASCESIS IS TRAINING

Hermit's hut (MG)

In Athos, where they understand both bodily and mental asceticism, I came to understand a different meaning for this word *ascesis*. In Christian context, *ascesis* is based on the teaching of St. Paul which says that, just as athletes must train for their contests, so the Christian must train for his Christianity – for without special training we lack the inner-strength to obey the commandments of Christ.

Because of this, asceticism may sometimes be the only true freedom-of-choice we possess, just as it was in many places after they had been conquered – for in the triumph of rationalism, modern-man has been conquered and his consciousness overcome by a flood of words. But my studies also suggest that there are also other times when the layman, if he is able, may take an alternative form of voluntary asceticism, a more internal-form, different from the monk's external asceticism. For this different asceticism, obedience is not enough. Real understanding is also necessary.

The underlying idea is perhaps best explained by what I was told by the Abbot of Gregoriou during my seventh visit. It was then that he answered a question which I had never put to him, but which had been on my mind for a very long time.

At the same time, he connected two previously-separated understandings of mine: One was the awareness that, although real spiritual growth is given by God, and only in response to a real wish or decision on the part of the individual, yet for all but the youngest of those on the spiritual path, these wishes must be very-clear to us before that help will be given.

My other question has been about the verbal part of the mind, which contemporary thought links – rightly or wrongly – to the so called 'dominant hemisphere' of the brain. This is the part of the brain that has been shown to play the major role in most everyday action – at least in Western man. It seems to be associated with 'learned and imitative actions.' Almost certainly, true humility is when this dominance of the 'verbal' mind comes to an end.

I had also, since first coming to Athos, become increasingly curious about the real role of asceticism. The early fathers of the Church taught a strict asceticism. The monks of Athos today practice a rigorous ascetical discipline. Yet in our comfortable West most people believe asceticism to be foolish. One can see why it is seen as foolish. Clearly there is something silly about doing unpleasant things for their own sake, yet in the West we have never understood the real reasons for asceticism.

It has become clear to me that on an essentially sane Athos, everything is done for the sake of God. Nothing unpleasant would be done 'for its own sake.' The blindness in the Western view of *ascesis* is indeed sad, because it became clear to me in this conversation that *ascesis*, if it is not properly understood, will produce little or no benefit.

TEST OF UNITY

What then is the point of asceticism? Father George explained it: *"God will help, will send the Holy Spirit to help, but only when you wish it more than anything else."* If we are wholehearted and humble about it, we may not be divided. This, as mentioned earlier, is what underlies the impression given by the Old Testament that its God was a jealous God.

This knowledge, the insight that *'God does not accept or respond to a divided heart,'* is part of the heritage which Christianity obtained from Judaism.

Wholeheartedness about what they are doing is what releases people from one-sided dominance by their mind and opens their heart to the Holy Spirit. *'What is needed,'* said the Abbot, *'is ascesis.'* We had a moment of difficulty with pronunciation: *ascesis* is a difficult word to pronounce clearly. He continued: *"Ascesis is how we show God that we have made our choice; it is how we choose. So it takes many forms.*

One gives-up comfort, one gives-up food, one gives-up sleep, one gives-up pleasure, one gives alms: this ascesis is the key to obtaining God's help; God's help is the key to spiritual growth. When we turn to God by means of ascesis, God turns towards us, gives us the help of the Holy Spirit, instructs us through the Holy Spirit, teaching us to pray more fully."

For layman as well as monk, then, the asceticism is the key that opens to us Christ's strait-and-narrow Way. It can take many forms. In the *Gerontikon*, so beloved in Athos, they tell the story of the sick monk who was lying on his back, his legs in the air. The same story is told by ascetics in India.

'Why are you waving your legs in the air?' They asked an old monk. "To get to God," he said, "you can do all kinds of practices, but all I can do is wave my legs."

Among the Early Fathers, different saints followed different forms of asceticism. It seems that it is not the kind of practice that matters, but the inner quality, shown in two things:

1. That to give up something for God – something we never wanted anyway – God, who knows the death of the sparrow and the toils of the human heart, will know when we short-change Him.

2. When we fulfill these conditions, then God through His Holy Spirit sends us the strength and the instruction we need. Thus, although on Athos there are certain proven forms of asceticism, different individuals, at different times, follow different ascetic forms.

The monastery food is one example of this 'general asceticism.' The early hour at which services begin – anything from 2 am onwards – is another. On one occasion, I was offered a monk's cell that contained two beds, and I first lay down to rest on the 'wrong' one ... hidden under a perfectly ordinary blanket were hard planks instead of a mattress. On Athos, cushions are almost unknown. In the external sense, too, a monk's pleasures are few. Also, asceticism often lies in acceptance, and true pilgrimage can become a contained form of asceticism. I have found this so on Athos, where on every visit to the Holy Mountain I have met again the same great difficulties at the beginning. These difficulties are of course in me.

If my experience is normal, they are in everyone. Each time my established habits of thought and action are aroused by what is happening, I meet again what I first met many years ago, a special kind of fear: fear of the emptiness that arises when one is without one's usual distractions. This for me – as probably for many – has proved a recurrent blockage to spirituality.

Going back to my third visit to Athos, in Autumn once again, this visit provided an extreme example of this pattern, and a real education in the asceticism of acceptance. My main aim this time was the wish to see for the first time the hermit Father Paisios, about whom I have already written.

This aim was in fact attained, but only right at the end of my time in Greece, very much at the last minute. Before this, my visit brought with it new and different difficulties, many of them of my own making, but exaggerated by the emptiness one feels on Athos before the sweetness described by St. Gregory of Nyssa arises. At one such time, several problems combined so that on one visit to Greece I had to make the entry to Athos on three separate occasions.

Only in this way was I finally able to achieve my several objectives: to stay with my many recent but greatly valued friends at Gregoriou; to visit more briefly the monks at Simonos Petra whom I had previously met and come to admire; and finally, to see this hermit, as suggested by an Orthodox priest in England. I had also hoped perhaps to visit the small monastery of Stavronikita, which had few beds for visitors, and which I had several times heard to be distinguished by its atmosphere of peace and tranquility.

But this I did not achieve on this third visit.

The journey to Greece had begun easily enough: a midweek flight with a packaged-tour company avoided the cost and discomfort of hanging around in Saloniki all weekend, waiting for papers.

When I called at the Ministry of Northern Greece for my Athos visa, there was only one other *'xenos'* present, an American whose main aim, as I later discovered, was to work with John Lilly and his dolphins. I had no difficulty getting a pass for the date I had selected. The same afternoon, we moved on directly to Ouranoupolis and the 'front door' of Athos.

Finally, after several days watching the number of holidaymakers dwindle, and seeing the selection offered by the waterfront-cafes of Ouranoupolis grow smaller day-by-day, the day of departure to Athos came. By now, the 'summer service' of two boats a day had ended, and only one boat left for Dafni some-time before 10 am each day.

"Now you have to stay in Karyes tonight," said Neboysha, our Yugoslavian friend from the American seminary

THUNDERSTORM

Next morning, as we waited, there was an impressive thunderstorm. However, when I finally went for the boat, there was still a great crowd on the jetty, and while we few non-Greek visitors waited for the harbor-police to collect our passports and allow us onto the boat, many monks and Greek pilgrims filled the seats. Among them, I noticed a familiar face, the bearded young Cypriot who had been so considerate and helpful on my last visit to Gregoriou. He saw me and smiled, and, when I finally got aboard the boat, beckoned me over to a seat beside him.

Soon the boat started off. On this morning the air was distinctly cool, the sky gray, and the sea a little choppy, making the smaller fishing boats 'porpoise' over the waves. As the boat set off, I watched for the sky to clear as it so often did in the mornings.

Instead, as we sailed along the Athonite shore towards the distant cone of the Holy Mountain itself at the tip of the peninsula, the clouds around the mountain appeared more and more pervasive.

It was soon apparent that they clung not only to the peak, but to the whole of the high 'spine' of the peninsula, and that they were slowly spreading towards the mainland.

The heart of this spreading cloud was dark and forbidding, and by the time we were half-way to Dafni, sheets of rain were seen in the distance, falling from the clouds that clung to the forested-ridge of the peninsula.

It was not long, it seemed, before the boat began to penetrate into the light-rain that formed the advance guard of the approaching storm. In ones and pairs and small groups, the crowded passengers began to pack themselves, with their cardboard-wrapped bundles and light packs, into the small cabin amidships on the caique. I hastened to join them. By the time we reached Dafni, the first rain had also reached the little port. Not expecting it, I had not brought rain-proof, or even waterproof, shoes. I considered returning on the same boat, but my passport and papers were by then en-route to Karyes, and my Greek was nowhere near good enough to explain my problem to their bearer. By the time I existed again as a legal-entity, the boat would be long-gone. I had no alternative but to join the crowd who were listlessly sheltering where they could, in shops, or under porches, to avoid the rain that by then poured, while we still waited to enter the bus which already stood on the quayside.

Some twenty minutes later, we crowded onto the ancient bus and began the slow crawl up the mountain to Karyes. The rain fell in sheets, and the shallow drainage channels alongside the roads had become raging mountain torrents. Below in the deep purple sea spread three great fans of yellow water. These enormous stains reached out some half-mile from their apexes on the shore, mute testimony to the rainwater's powers of eroding the topsoil. The bus slowed several-times to ford streams that had over-topped their concrete channels and flooded across the un-metalled road.

We arrived in Karyes without mishap, and spread-out in damp procession along the rough and now-muddy streets of the little town. I headed towards the police station to regain my passport, only to be stopped by a middle-aged Greek, who authoritatively asked me: *'Foreign?"* I agreed I was. *"First to Holy Community."* He pointed to the high steps of the council house opposite the Protaton church.

I said something about having to obtain my passport first, but he insisted: *"Holy Community first."*

Wrongly assuming that perhaps methods had changed since the Spring, I followed his advice, and went up the steps into the Holy Community building, where people were beginning to wait, everyone crowded together on one side of the hall. The little glass kiosk under the stairs remained empty.

Finally, some half-hour later, a monk appeared in the kiosk, and the line of pilgrims began to shuffle forward. I crept with them. Eventually, reaching the window, I asked for a *diamonitirion.*

"Papers?" Said the monk from behind his glass barrier. *"From the police."* I left the queue, put on my jacket again, shouldered my bag, and crossed the square to the police-station, which was of course locked and deserted. Even the cardboard sign in English, which had been there a few months before, had vanished. Was this still the police station, or was it not? Had I forgotten? Had it been moved? Of such minor problems the pilgrim's day is made. I looked into the hotel next door.

"Police?" I asked. Nobody understood. Finally, one of them went to fetch the proprietor.

"You want room?" He asked hopefully. *"No,"* I told him, just my passport. His smile faded, but he gestured towards the door I had just vacated. I again went up the stairs and looked through the glass door of the corner room on the landing. Nobody there! But behind me a policeman in shirt-sleeves came round the corner, asked me something in Greek. When I said to him: *"Passport."* He said, *"Okay,"* unlocked the door of the office, and went in.

In less than a minute, I had my papers, and was on my way back to the Holy Community, where I rejoined the queue, by now a little shorter. By this time it was, if I remember aright, around twelve-thirty, and I had not yet managed to learn what chance there was of reaching the monastery of Gregoriou that day.

"What time is the bus back to Dafni?" I hopefully asked my Cypriot friend, to be told that there would be no bus that day. The torrential rain had become a thunderstorm that circled round flashing overhead and echoing-off the mountains. On this night, I must stay in Karyes, a daunting prospect. What should I do?

192

KONACHI

At this point, the magic of Athos came to my rescue, as it sometimes does. My Cypriot friend, guessing my dilemma, told me that he was staying the night in the Gregoriou house or 'konachi' at Karyes. (As previously mentioned, each of the twenty main monasteries has a konachi or residence for its representative at Karyes, inside or just outside this little capital.)

Knowing my connection with the monastery, he suggested that I too should be welcome there. When we had our papers, we walked off down one of the narrow paths that thread their winding way between the houses of Karyes; past garden-walls of rich colored stone, vine-covered loggias, rusted iron gates and simple fences the path led, the long grass at the sides tangled and dripping; a tiny and complex world of its own. *"I hope this is the way,"* said my friend. *"I have been there before."* The path grew narrower, the soaked grass and weeds thicker. Few people had been this way in some weeks, at least. *"It is not here!"* He said. We retraced our steps to the last junction on the edge of the town.

"This way, I think." We began walking again, between two tall buildings in regular blocks of red sandstone, built right up to the track. Then we turned down the side of one, and again found ourselves between two-walls. This time, the track was better-used. It led us down into the woods, where the paths were filled with plump fresh chestnuts, waiting for someone to come by and pick them up. At a gap in one of the walls, we turned through a rough 'turnstile' gate, a type they sometimes use on Athos, and walked past a low stone building, half-hidden in trees, then through a wooden gate, left open, which we fastened behind us. The rain continued. We crossed a small wooden bridge and continued under the chestnuts. Soon, we saw a long, low house before us, so low that we were arriving almost at roof level. We followed a muddy track down to the small courtyard at the front of the house, and pulled the bell.

For several minutes, nothing happened. The thunder continued to rumble away in the hills. Then the door opened and a young monk looked out. My friend greeted him in Greek.

We were ushered in where the door opened on a great dark hall-way forty or fifty feet long. Rooms opened off the sides and both ends.

We were shown where to hang our coats, and were offered dry clothing. Then we were shown down a short corridor. At the end was a toilet and washroom, with a big gray stone sink ... and behind the sink a long window, opening onto the wet-green chestnut woods. Through a door to the left was a room with table, chairs, and long blanket-covered ottomans. We were taken into this room, which had a magnificent view over the treetops in a little valley, and up to the high hills beyond, giving fascinating glimpses through the trees of a ruined and deserted monastic building considerably larger than the one we were in.

We sat for a few minutes, and another, older monk arrived, Father A, who I had seen before at Gregoriou. Everyone talked for a few minutes. Then the younger monk went off to prepare food for the unexpected visitors. The older man too disappeared, and I heard him talking on the telephone. A few minutes later he returned. It was alright, I could stay the night. After a simple meal we were shown to simple rooms overlooking the soaking forest, and left to rest.

Through it all, the thunder had been passing over and return-ing. Now it built again to a crescendo near where we were staying. During one flash there was a bang from inside the house, from the telephone. Other thunderbolts sounded all round, and each rumbled briefly along the ridge and through the surrounding hills. The storm seemed to remain right on top of us for hours, and what rest I had was fitful and nervous. Is it that lightning seems worse in strange surroundings? Finally it passed over. Sunshine broke-through briefly.

There was a tap on my door: my Cypriot friend again. He was going to take advantage of the break in the weather to take a walk around the gardens, would I like to join him? Some two minutes or so later, we were picking our way under the grapevines surrounding the house on loggias, and so across an unused area of garden. The path led into the woods, and to a small circular stone seat with a simple roof.

Beyond it, the woods looked as they must have looked before ever the monks came to Athos, green, still, empty. We stopped there briefly in the dripping silence, and then, as the afternoon light began to fade and the rain began again, picked our way back, wet of foot, over a bank to the front door of the house. As we entered, there was a great flurry of marmalade kittens on the steps, most vocal proof that the regulations on Athos are more flexible for cats than for man.

I returned to my room to lie down for a little longer. By now my stomach was reacting to the strain, the long exposure to the rain, and to the unfamiliar food of the past few days with all the symptoms of a chill.

We waited an hour or so, and then, as the last light faded and the rain returned with thunder once again, we were called to a short evening-service in the chapel. In a way that I have been told is typical of Athos *kellia*, this chapel opened through double doors onto the main-hall of the house, allowing many people to attend services.

APOCALYPSE

Icons illuminated (MG)

There were only six of us there in the gloom, and in the small chapel itself were just ten stalls of the usual Athos misericordia type.

A few small candles gave tantalizing glimpses of the most magnificent carved wooden iconostasis, crowded with age-darkened icons and ornate (but not at all bright) lamps. The younger of the two monks pulled down and lit the cone-shaded lamp by the simple reader's desk, throwing a circle of dim yellow light on the service books, and began reading from the litany.

Between them, the two monks and my Cypriot friend – invited to help them read – completed the whole service in an atmosphere of simplicity and peace, just as it would have been said in the monastery, except that, throughout the service, the thunder and the blue flashes of the lightning crept closer again.

After this service, at about eight-thirty, we again went to the room with the long-ottomans, now lit by a hissing gas-lamp with a conical black metal shade. The storm was by now in its ninth hour. Outside, the last gleams of evening-light were regularly eclipsed by the flashes of lightning. Everyone then spent a short time drinking tea. After checking out the telephone – also 'eclipsed' by the lightening – they began talking about religious ideas. I could not follow them, despite occasional efforts by the others to translate a particularly significant statement. All I could gather was that one or two of those present – there were now two Greek civilians as well as the two monks, my companion, and myself – were amongst those whose concern with the state of the world today has firmed into a quite definite expectation of apocalypse. Perhaps they were expressing the mood shaped by the thunderstorm … which seemed to rotate around the little hilltop valley of Karyes, unable to pass the barrier of the mountains behind.

NIGHT IN THE STORM

The rain poured down, and the rumbling and the flashes continued, hour after hour. Typically, I attempted in my very English way, fortunately limited by my lack of Greek, to suggest that a wider-view was possible, and that it was dangerous to dramatize. But dramatic places perhaps encourage dramatic thinking.

Athos certainly has sometimes a power for creating exaggerated behavior, as well as a power for creating powerful manifestations of spirituality!

After a while we dispersed to bed in the light of the small glass oil-lamp in each room. I quickly fell into a disturbed sleep, to be woken whenever the thunder again grew louder. Sometime in the early morning my sleep became unbroken, until I was woken about five for morning service. Not quite as early as the monasteries, the small house nevertheless maintained the typical Athos early-morning routine. This time, the service was quite clearly led by the elder of the two monks.

In the absence of a priest, no full liturgy was possible, but the service ended with each participant taking a piece of the *'antidoron'* bread and a sip of consecrated water, both stored in a niche by the door of the chapel.

Then there was a light meal – bread, feta cheese, an apple. By now the thunder had finally dispersed but rain still fell heavily. Because of the continued heavy rain I was invited to stay over until the next day. Rain is relatively uncommon on Athos, and when it occurs few people travel. However, my stomach upset of the night before had definitely turned into a chill, and I decided that rather than make problems for myself and my hosts on the Holy mountain I should return for a couple of days to regain my strength in Ouranoupolis, and then try to visit my friends at Gregoriou when I was more my normal self.

"What time does the bus go?" I asked. About 11, I was told, as the elder of the two monks left the house – umbrella overhead – to the Holy Community building and his day's work as his monastery's representative on the Council that governs this little theocracy.

RETURN TO OURANOUPOLIS

The service had taken some time. I packed my small bag, tided my room, and made my farewells. There was less than an hour before the bus, as I made my slow way up the muddy path, over the little-bridge, and finally along the main track between its stone walls and so into the town.

I hoped on the way to obtain certain items I had promised to friends in England; wooden-crosses, prayer-ropes, a few gifts with the unique-significance of things made and bought on the Holy Mountain. So I went into the first shop, empty but for a selection of carved wooden items, prayer-ropes, crosses and icons. I did not find what I wanted, and moved on, past the cobbler-monk in his little shop, and the tailor-monk – a big man in untidy robes, walking down the street with rain on his glasses and wearing his tape measure round his neck like a stole.

Opposite the little hotel, there were three more shops that, in typical Greek fashion, sell a little of everything.

In them, you can buy maps, tinned meat, torches, oil-lamps, biscuits by the hundredweight, oil and vinegar in the little soft plastic bottles you see in many monasteries, soft-drinks which, from the look of the quayside at Dafni, are Athos' major import, although I have never seen them in the monasteries.

No luck. The few crosses I could see seemed too expensive for my purpose. The prayer-ropes available were very complicated and colorful, obviously designed for tourists – as were the prices, which reached a peak at that visit, so that some prayer-ropes cost nearly ten-pounds. It seems difficult to grudge the money, when some of the hermits support themselves frugally just by making prayer-ropes, but it would certainly limit one's ability to give them as gifts. Later evidence suggests that Western ways have penetrated Athos, and that somebody other than the makers was reaping the profit. By now, people were gathering round the bus, and I had to join them to be sure of a place. On the way, I noticed at the side of the square the sacking-covered engine which had been removed from the bus during my previous trip. It was still laying where it had been put six-months before.

I got onto the bus with the rest of the waiting throng, monks and Greek visitors, finding a seat before it became too crowded. With the cutback to one boat had been a cut to one bus a day, so that the ending of the tourist season had left the bus as crowded as was normal during the peak season. After a considerable wait, the driver's assistant began collecting payment and distributing tickets. Finally, we started off on the downhill journey to Dafni.

I had an uncomfortable journey back, and after leaving the boat, which was one of the smaller boats of those that make the run, and was crowded, I walked to the house where we had rooms, finding Lillian having lunch with our landlady.

Then I had all the difficulties of explaining that I had been forced to return without seeing Father Paisios, and even without visiting my friends at Gregoriou. I would rest, and then perhaps try again while my papers still permitted. But I was not yet sure about that.

"Nico has caught some fish." I was told. *"Do you want some?"* Such kindness! But I could not face more fish.

SECOND ATTEMPT

Athos in the clouds (MG)

It required three-nights back in Ouranoupolis before I felt well enough to visit the mountain again for the little-time remaining on my six-day registration. When I woke and prepared for the trip, the weather was fine, if slightly overcast. There was a light swell on the Aegean. Again the boat was crowded, the morning cool.

We stopped at every jetty along the coast, until we finally came to Dafni, nosing into the quay as the bus came down the hill from Karyes trailing a plume of dust. Since I already had my paperwork sorted, I had no need to go to Karyes, so as the bus loaded with visitors for Karyes, and the *caique* with monks who could go immediately from one boat to another and along the coast to their destinations, I adjusted the weight of my bag on my shoulder. Then, looking suspiciously at the clouds round Athos herself, I began for a third-time the long climb from Dafni to Simonos Petra.

I first passed the monastery's timber-warehouse and yard, just behind the buildings of Dafni, then began to walk along the long dirt-road up the mountainside. As I moved up the slope, I heard first the Ouranoupolis ferry, and then the *caique* start up; one big engine, one little thumper putt-putting across the water.

The ferry cut like an arrow across the bay, back towards the outside world, the *caique* slowly pulled out to sea, and in a few minutes, passed below me as it moved up the coast. This time, there were few flowers. The exposed parts of the road were dry, but the sheltered sections and the drainage-channels showed signs of recent-soaking. Recently cut channels in the sand, and water-deposited deltas of sandy-soil spread along or across the road in many places, marked by few recent tracks. Nobody else was walking. As the boat engines faded into the distance a great silence – the silence of Athos – fell over the whole mountain.

Remembering how tired I could be if I rushed the climb, and how this would make me forget my purpose in coming to the mountain, I made a plan. I would climb for ten minutes, then stop and pray the Jesus-prayer for twenty-five knots on the prayer rope. Then I would climb again. Then, in my typical English fashion, I would stop halfway up, make tea, and have a light lunch. Afterwards, I would continue in the same way as at the beginning.

And so I did, for an uneventful climb, until I reached a deep soak-away beside the road some thousand feet above the sea. In the soak-away were the prints of large paws, fresh and recent. Yet there had been no tracks on the way up and, as I soon discovered, were none beyond.

All the recent scare-stories about wolves on the mountain came back to my imagination, made fertile by uncertainty and over-activity. I walked on nervously. Were these paw-prints not too small for wolves?

I thought they must be – but could not be sure, having never seen a wolf except on television.

After another ten minutes of walking, and another stop for prayer as I crossed a small concrete bridge – I heard a repeated irregular sound some distance behind me: tap tap tap, tap tap tap, tap tap, tap tap... dull, like sticks being tapped together. What was it?

It was not a sound I recognized. Soon it was joined by another, then another. I heard animal growls. More and more puzzled, I walked back a short way to the point where I could see down a long straight section of road. Round the bend at the far end came a big dark-brown dog, then three more; a small pack hunting up the road. Suddenly I remembered where I had heard that tapping sound before. The previous Autumn in Ouranoupolis, there had been a young dog with a bell.

The tap-tapping of this bell had come and gone all through the night beside the house where we were then staying, so that I had made considerable effort to find out what caused it. Now, here were four great dogs with these wooden bells. The paw prints were explained. The strange noise was explained. I was not really so certain that the dogs were explained, but some few minutes later, the lead dog turned off into the woods, followed by the others. I never saw their owner, nor ever heard them again. Almost certainly, they were hunting-dogs, but what were they hunting: boar, or wolves, or smaller game?

I stopped again for prayer, and then continued – by now somewhat slowed – on my way around the high sloping side of Athos toward Simonos Petra on its steep rock. Then came a period familiar to Athos travelers. Each time I walked round a bend to see a new section of the mountainside, I would think: *"This time I shall see the monastery."* Each time, I would be disappointed. Eventually, it happened. There, as I came round a corner, was the prominent shape of Simonos Petra against the skyline. Above it, Holy Athos reared its marble-streaked head into the surrounding cloud. The path by now ran downhill, and the going was easier. I took a sip of water, and continued.

HARALAMBOS AGAIN

Again the monastery was hidden as the path curved back into the convex mountainside. Then I passed the last bend, and there before me was the final long, curving slope that leads to the monastery itself ... and below me, the door of Saint Simon's cave. Above, too, were buildings, houses high up the hillside; working-buildings beside the stream; a Roman-looking aqueduct that showed by how-many-centuries the monastery then predated modern plumbing.

Far below, the sea looked motionless, although I knew this to be untrue. Somewhere nearby, there was a distant sound of falling-water. Nobody moved. From this height, even the sea seemed smooth and still. I continued along the path in a deserted world, down the track to the foot of Saint Simon's rock, and the beginning of the gloomy tunnel up to the monastery courtyard. Eventually I arrived, panting, in the small bright courtyard, and made my way to the final wooden staircase up to the guest house.

There once again, I met the still-smiling face of young Father Haralambos. Had that smile been there all the time since my last visit? Looking at him, I could well believe it.

Haralambos was now *archontarios* or guest-master, and busy learning English from any guest who could help, unlike the previous guest-master, who would try to make me speak the French at which he himself was so bad. So on this visit to Simonos Petra, I was assured of a welcome, although sure about little else. The angelic Father D was away.

That evening, my English friend Father I was able to find a little time to talk, and we spoke this time about England. He was very disappointed by his country, and spoke about his doubts about English religion. It was this which had caused him to leave his country.

He would have liked to come with me to visit Father Paisios, but was unable to leave the monastery. He spoke about a recent visit he had made to the Ecumenical Patriarch in Constantinople, and the problems this had caused.

I gained the impression that after this show of initiative he was under some pressure to be a little 'less English' in his ways of doing things.

In these conversations, nothing of real importance emerged: they served a different function, of establishing a deeper level of respect, the basis, I hope and suspect, of a lasting friendship.

Sadly, too little time was available. Night fell, and with the fading of the colorful sunset over the hills of Sithonia across the silent sea, the monastery slipped into silence, and I to my bed in the guest-dormitory, reminiscent of an English boarding-school.

DEPARTURE FOR GREGORIOU

The next day I hoped to continue my conversation, but Father I was unable to join me on the balcony as he had intended. Because I had little time left on my *diamonitirion,* I must push on that day for Gregoriou if I hoped to complete my visit. I had no more time to rest legs unaccustomed to such exertions. Eventually, mid-morning, I picked up my bags, said adieu to Father Haralambos, still with his perpetual smile – and left down the tunnel, through the archway where the mules were stabled in winter, and on down the steep mule-track towards the picturesque monastery of St. Gregory: towards my friends living far away from all roads but, I was convinced, in some sense nearer to God for this fact.

Walking slowly, with frequent rests because of the weakness of my legs, I arrived by the jetty below Gregoriou in time to hear the semantron clattering in the distance, and then had to make my way as quickly as I could up the slope, past the familiar pine-tree with its seat overlooking the cove below, then under the vine-covered loggia before the gate, and, crossing myself to the icon, into the gates of the monastery.

From there, I found my way through the courtyard, and up the steps with ten minutes to leave my bags, take the obligatory coffee and raqi, and fill in the visitors book, all in the monastery's *archontaria,* the guest house reception-room built out almost directly over the ocean.

After this, it was time to move back across the courtyard, crossing myself as I followed arriving monks into the familiar friendly gloom of the monastery church and finding a creaking stall at the back of the narthex.

Here and there, a familiar face would smile, nod, or bow his tented head lightly, hand on heart, in silent greeting. I was among friends, and as I allowed myself to fall still, I could see right up the center of the Katholikon to the royal doors of the sanctuary, with the golden light of candles shining off the polished-brass of chandelier, candlestick, staff and finial. From the gloom on either side came the chanting of the monks with its Byzantine, almost Asiatic, quality. The service had begun.

From the Katholikon, the way led as-usual straight into the *trapeza* for the evening meal, symbolizing the link between body and spirit. From there to the courtyard again to wait for Compline, the last service of the day. Now the greetings came. Smiles and nods from the monks who did not speak English. Father S bowing with his broad grin, so that I awaited his next weak-joke, almost forgetting that he did not speak my language. Then Father P came up to me.

"You are very welcome." His smile showed this to be so. *"Have you come from Karyes today?"*

"No," I told him, *"From Simonos Petra."*

I explained what had happened to my plans.

CHAPTER 17

LEARNING HUMILITY

Pirgos - Ouranoupolis (MG)

On this confused trip to Greece, I came back from my second visit to the Holy Mountain after five days at the monasteries of Simonas Petra and Gregoriou. I hadn't been able to get to Father Paisios, as I couldn't find an interpreter. But I was happy because I had found something of what I went for; answers enough to hint at how to resolve the emotional question, even if I had not yet learned to do so in practice, and was still only beginning to find the peace I sought. I had by now more or less accepted that I wouldn't see Father Paisios this time, as my *diamonitirion* or Athos visa allowed me only six days, and would expire as I returned.

So if I was to see this remarkable man, I believed, I should have to wait until next time I could make the long journey to Greece. But where Athos is concerned, things don't often work the way one expects. There does seem a certain sequence in things, however. You make your effort to make things happen, often with no visible result.

Then, just when you give up, when you say it is impossible, I can do nothing, coincidence taps on the door and says: it is all arranged. Go now! So the very nature of Greece conspires with truth, with God perhaps, to make one a little more humble. Is it coincidence? Around Athos, nobody is sure. It is as if something is trying to make a lesson clear, and around Athos things are a little more transparent, lessons a little more apparent. It certainly seemed clear, on this visit, that the results were out of my hands and in the hands of Him I sought. But later, back in England, it is easy again to doubt.

This third-voyage within a single trip to Greece began with great efforts made by others, after I had almost given up. That evening, it was the efforts of Maria, niece of Fani, landlady of our tiny Ouranoupolis apartment and, until the previous year, cook to Joyce Loch, the Australian-widow of Sidney Loch, now living alone in the *Pirgos*, the village's ancient monastic-tower beside the quay from which the boats leave for Agion Oros every day. In conversation, Maria mentioned that she was friendly with the Abbot of Xeropotamou, which we then thought, wrongly, to be the monastery closest to Father Paisios and so the best source for an interpreter. This seemed a great coincidence. So maybe something was possible in this way. We dropped by her house in the village that afternoon, as she was 'Autumn-Cleaning' during the holiday, and could be clearly seen in the house, originally built to a standard plan when her parents, with many other villagers, were forcibly evacuated from Asia-Minor in the 1920's. She invited us in for *'kaffe hellenika,'* and we told her that I had been advised by an English priest to see Father Paisios, and that I had not so far found it possible.

Could the Abbot of Xeropotamou help, and could she put in a word for us? (Things in Greece run very often on this basis. Among these friendly people, a word from a friend is worth a great deal!) Immediately she went to the telephone, trying several times, in case services had not yet ended at the monastery. Finally, she called another friend in the Athos capital of Karyes, repeated the story in detail, and asked advice. She was told to ask the local Harbor Police, so she decided to see them herself.

In the meantime, she suggested that we take a planned trip to the Island of Amoulani, the small but beautiful island tucked down between the bases of the two 'fingers' of Athos and Sithonia, and clearly in-sight from Ouranoupolis.

ATTEMPTS TO RETURN

When we returned that evening she greeted us jubilantly. She had told the Harbor Police the whole story over the 'phone, and they said there should be no problem. Just to make sure, we decided we should all three visit them before Sunday, the day when I was to go back to the mountain, because on Saturday there would be many weekend-pilgrims going in.

We agreed to go in on the Saturday night before the sailing. The weather throughout this visit was very changeable. Often the finger of Athos, rising six thousand foot straight from the sea, divided the clouded weather flowing down from the North like a zip-fastener, clouds to the left, sunshine to the right.

On Saturday, it was a hot, muggy day that could have been Salonika at the beginning of September. By the end of the day, I was feeling quite shaky again, but we decided it was too late to back down now we had 'got the whole town going.' So on Saturday night, we went down the lane, and up the outside staircase to the Harbor Police Office over *'Steve's Restaurant, Best Fish, Best Prices.'* A strange officer was there, recently 'rotated' from another part of Greece. He had never spoken to Maria.

The 'boss' would be out until Monday ... so come back then. Persistently, she said that I intended to go in Sunday so, after much to-ing and fro-ing, he said that if we came down early Sunday, he would see if the senior man on-duty could help. A little light, but pretty well back to square one!

That night the weather changed again. Again we slept little, because of the noise of the waves, breaking just across the road from the house. In the morning, the sea was high, the sky dark, and the fishing-boats still in port. Over Athos, the clouds were ominous ... it might get better, it might be heading for another day-long thunderstorm ... we didn't know the local weather well enough to guess.

Seacoast of Athos (MG)

On Athos, most travel stops when it is like that, but the visitor to where Father Paisios was located may not be as lucky as others. At weekends, the load of tourists and pilgrims to this small village of monks is too great for Greek hospitality to maintain its customary smile for the stranger. As nothing had been arranged about accommodation or interpreter, and as I was not feeling very fit, I was dubious about making the trip. The idea of another hike in an Athos downpour with no proper waterproofs did not appeal at all.

When Maria left Church to come with us to the quay, we were beginning to have qualms of conscience about all she was doing for us. It is like this in Greece; you ask a question, and things are set in motion that must grind inexorably to their conclusions. We told her about my doubts, and agreed anyway to go to see the Harbor Police.

When we got through the near-gale to an almost-deserted quay, we found yet another new face who knew – once again – nothing about the previous discussions.

Finding no response, and getting a little frayed around the edges, we said we'd try again on Monday, and left to reach the church just in time to hear the long sermon (in Greek) with which the service ended. We were at least able to collect some Blessed Water that Maria had not been able to wait for earlier.

Monday woke cold, but with a calm sea and a shining sky. We started the day with my bag packed, and a good breakfast more in hope than expectation, and picked up Maria around nine – somewhat harassed, as her father had been taken sick in the night.

We found the senior Harbor-Policeman, but none of them seemed to know much of what had gone before, so they helpfully let Maria tell our story for the fourth time. The 'boss' said that as far as he was concerned, it was OK, but he had to check with the monastery, which was the final arbiter. We had by-now realized that, confused by all the strange names, I had got it wrong, and that it was a different monastery, on the other side of Karyes, which should be contacted. They were telephoned, but, being close to Karyes and with few monks, were not too helpful.

Once again, Maria kept the ball rolling. There was still half an hour before the boat, she told us. Kyria Fani was friendly with a high-official at Karyes. Perhaps she could help. We rushed back along the coast road, Maria jogging alongside us. Fani tried to phone but the lines were jammed. She and Maria were arguing over which number might be best to try, (the only time we saw either of them lose their tempers, Maria being a younger version of Fani, who, after years of catering for sometimes aged, and if they are anything like me, very-demanding 'Anglicos' pilgrims, has aged into a wonderfully selfless person).

LAST CHANCE

The situation seemed hopeless. Fani had finally got through to someone, but no one who could help, when somebody drove up to the door and asked for Niko, her son. Lillian's immediate reaction was to avoid this last-minute interruption by telling them that Niko was just then driving down the street.

But one of the men overheard the conversation as it ended. *"Give me the phone,"* he said, reaching through the door. He was in his thirties, smartly dressed in a corduroy-suit. He asked for the senior man Fani had tried unsuccessfully to contact. In two minutes, it was all settled. He said a few words to Fani in Greek, then went out to a car-phone to inform the Harbor Police. Suddenly, the Greek kaleidescope had shifted, and we were in a different world once again.

Grabbing that hastily packed bag, we rushed for the Harbor Office, meeting the police en-route as they headed for the quay. At the quay, the man in dark glasses and corduroy shook my hand, and said in good English: *"Okay, you can stay for two days if you want."* He boarded the boat. Neboysha was right behind us. *"That chap must have some clout,"* said Lillian. *"You bet,"* said Neboysha. *"He's the governor of Athos."*

COMMUNICATION PROBLEMS

"After senseless sense pleasures," said one of the Early Fathers, *"comes pain."*

This time, when I reached Karyes, I was to meet new problems. Firstly, I still did not have an interpreter, and the geron I was supposed to meet spoke only Greek. Secondly, I did not have anywhere to stay. Kindheartedly, Neboysha had suggested an answer to both these problems ... the same answer to both, his friend, the 'Protos' or senior-monk for that year – another of the three governors – was a Serbian monk who spoke English. He was living in his Karyes residence, the Serbian konachi, but during services, I could find him at the Protaton, the big thousand-year-old communal church at the center of Karyes. Neboysha wrote a note for me to take to his influential friend.

As soon as I arrived in Karyes, and had completed one or two errands, such as buying crosses for a priest in England, I began to look for the *Protos*. Once again, my lack of Greek held me up. *"Protos?"* I asked one monk.

He answered in Greek that I could not translate, then shook his head at my inability and departed. I approached another with much the same results.

I went up the wide story-high flight of steps of the Holy Community Building, and asked the ecclesiastical policeman with his beret and brass 'A-O' badge (AO for 'Agion-Oros'). He shook his head. Not here! Then I asked a third monk, who turned out to be an American. *"Too late,"* he told me. *"Siesta time. He has gone to sleep for the afternoon."* He walked on about his shopping. It was by now well into the afternoon. The rough street of the little town was almost deserted. The shops were beginning to put up their afternoon-shutters.

I spied a dark-skinned youngster who had come from Ouranoupolis on the same boat, now walking into the ground floor of one of the two ramshackle 'hotels' with his companion, an aged priest with long white beard. Half an hour later, I met him again, on the road.

"Still here?" he asked, in perfect English with a slight Australian accent. We spoke for a few minutes, walking along the street until we could see the distant peak of Athos over the tops of the buildings. He said he and his Abbot – who was with him – were going to stay in the hotel, and suggested I do the same. Eventually I decided to do so, and went to the proprietor to arrange a bed for the night. The cost was 20 drachmas, then worth about one pound eighty ... for a bed in a small room with three other beds, two of them already occupied by young men, one of them with tape recorder.

BITTER WATERS

On every visit to Athos, I have at some time rediscovered this *'well of bitter waters'* that was first described by the Fathers of the Church so long ago. But then, in the monasteries, there is a palliative for this unease: as St. Gregory of Nyssa put it, they possess the wood of the cross, symbolic of the living-liturgy, which sweetens the bitterness. Here, I am now convinced, is medicine for this internal sensation.

"After crossing the day's march, and during this time they encamped in a place where they found water which they could not at first drink because of its bitter taste.

"But the wood that Moses cast into the water made it a pleasant drink for them in their thirst.

"The text corresponds to what actually happens; when a man has given up the Egyptian pleasures to which he had been enslaved before crossing the water, his life seems at first bitter and disagreeable now his pleasures have been taken away. But once the wood is cast into the waters, that is, once he unites himself to the mystery of the resurrection, which had its beginning in the wood – and by the wood here you surely understand the Cross – then the life of virtue becomes sweeter and more refreshing than all the sweetness that makes the senses tingle with pleasure, because it has been seasoned by our hope in things to come." (St. Gregory of Nyssa's *Life of Moses,* Classics of Western Spirituality)

Four iron beds, four rickety chairs, pillow, blanket, a small table, an oil-lamp and several tacked up postcards of icons made up the furnishings. *"Like monastery,"* said the owner optimistically. I lay down, drew the blanket over my head and attempted to take my siesta. It was around three in the afternoon, and the day seemed to stretch interminably before me. It was during this long day, with no monastic spirituality to compensate for the barren environment, that I met in full-strength the *'bitter waters'* of separation from the distractions of the outside world, and so learned something about how, in our Western world, we use our comforts, our distractions to hide from ourselves. At the same time, I learned to value more-fully the unique riches of the monastic world which had been so-kindly opened to me.

At times like this – no matter what the external circumstance – the pattern is always the same. I would first face the freewheeling thoughts of my own mind, and then, when I managed to step back from these thoughts that continued to run through my head, I would meet this emptiness, this bitterness that emerges when one faces an immediate future that is not only without pleasures and without distractions, but also offers no certainty of something to replace those distractions. Then, if I would persist too long, would come anger.

Always, it is only after withstanding this inner-desert for a day, or even for several-days, that I discover once again the inner well of peace and happiness that makes it possible for the monk to live his hard and outwardly unrewarding life. So much does the effect of our ordinary life cling, that this benefit has often emerged only towards the end of a visit. From this experience I even began to see – just a little – how to obey the instruction mentioned elsewhere that had been given to St. Silouan. Properly understood, it provides a means to combat pride, the greatest of the passions and cause of our subordination to the active and verbal part of the mind. It is the key to that special form of mental asceticism needed by the *dikaios* who cannot fully indulge in external asceticism. It should be added here that some physical asceticism is still necessary, if perhaps only to show the body who is its master.

About our Western world, I began to see – more and more clearly – something that I had heard before: that we surround ourselves with people and things to fill our day. That we cannot live without these distractions: without our luxury foods, our cups of tea, our newspapers and our books, our 'chats,' our entertainments. Often, even our religious-activities, and even the important-tasks that fill our days, are nothing more than this attempt to calm ourselves, to keep the 'bitter-waters' away.

Away from my own controlled and ordered personal world, and cut-off from the opportunity of continual-conversation to fill the void, I learned quickly that I, like everyone, fill my days as if we are hiding from something. Then, when all the distractions are left behind, we are left face to face with ourselves, and then we must face our lack of emotional resources. It is then that a strange uneasiness wells up in us, as the wheels of our mind continue to turn with nowhere to go, nothing to relate to ... It is then that the emptiness of so much of our thought becomes – perhaps for the first time – actually visible to us.

The habit of activity, when it truly lacks somewhere to go, is so obviously pointless that the absence of distraction can actually become painful. One becomes aware of an absence of God, an absence of purpose, the lack of something essential at the heart of one's life; becomes conscious of one's forgetfulness of our redeemer,

He Who should be present with one always; Whose memory should be kept in our heart.

If this relates to the way we are normally dominated by the one hemisphere of the brain, as it seems to be, then this dominance is a dominance invited by us to hide the hollowness within us: a dominance to fill desperation. This, of course, explains a great part of the monastic discipline. The *Gerontikon* tells of a monk whose mind would wander, and who was greatly troubled by this. His *geron* told him to stay in his cell and do little but continue to pray. Slowly, the level of distraction reduced, and he found peace of mind. Sadly, to complete this kind of 'cold-turkey' treatment is not possible for those with too many responsibilities in the world.

Today, one's 'flight from Egypt' must be made on a return ticket. Then again, one seeks distraction. Pride emerges, we forget ourselves thoroughly, and so the eternal-circle continues as before.

6 PM PROTATON

Church interior (MG)

On this day, relief came at about 6:30 pm, when the bell at the *Protaton* church began to ring. Happy to be rescued, and welcoming any distraction, I crept from my room, down the rusty wrought-iron staircase on the side of the building, through the equally rusty gate, and in through the side door of the magnificent old church.

There were few there for the service that day: three or four old monks, and half a dozen young ones keeping to the rear ... the whole congregation lost in the great building, without the vitality of the monastery-churches. I sat in one of the stalls near the door, not realizing that the *Protos* was not at the service. Finally, when the service ended, I caught up with a group of the younger monks as they trooped out of the door.

"Protos", I queried once again. Courteously they smiled and called out to another young monk, tall and distinctive looking, who came over to me. *"Who do you want?"* he asked.

"Protos," I repeated once again, as always regretting how very slowly I was learning Greek. I handed him Neboysha's note. He smiled. *"Come,"* he said, *"Konachi! We find him."* We walked up the hill between the buildings, past the imposing 'OTE' telephone office with its chugging generator. Up a narrow lane between a big house and an unkempt stone walled garden.

Between wall and house, branches overhung and grape vines drooped from timbers. This was a strange lane; between it and the wall lay a wide ditch, some eight foot wide and the same depth. At the bottom, a stream trickled. Beside it, like a web, some seven or eight black plastic pipes of the do-it-yourself kind used all over Europe. Somewhere in the distance, a pump pulsed. I began to see the simple way in which the town organized its services.

Then we turned up another alley, rough slabs of stone at a steep angle between two rows of buildings. Halfway up, we stopped, and my guide knocked on an ornate but weather-beaten door. For two or three minutes we waited, then the door creaked open and another young monk looked out.

They talked together. *"Come,"* said my guide again, walking into the whitewashed passage beyond the door. Soon, this opened onto a small courtyard. The younger monk went to get a key.

My guide pointed out through a window to a tiny garden, perhaps six foot by eight, where there was an ornately painted wooden cross. This had been the home of a very saintly elder, he explained, and now his 'children' kept it up. Would I like to visit the chapel?

I would, and so the key just fetched opened the door onto a tiny-chapel, typical of many with which Karyes abounds. I stopped to pray, and then briefly to look, to pay my respects to the absent 'master' of the house. From the description, this might well have been the same chapel which Robert Byron and his friends in the 1920's so badly mistreated in their photographic zeal. Certainly it had some fine-frescoes: but frescoes were not then my concern, which was directed towards the living-starets in the forest.

Later reading has raised a question in my mind: *'Do English visitors to the Holy Mountain today still have to live down the youthful follies of that generation of idle-rich in their between-the-wars madness?'* It sometimes seems like it.

From this chapel, with its aura of devotion and the very tiny community around it, my guide led me yet further up the hill, along mule tracks and under the ever-present chestnut trees and a great fig tree. Finally, we came to the end of a lane, an iron gate onto a leveled terrace in front of a tall three-story house. On the terrace, a group of ancient chairs surrounded a stone table, with a canopy to keep off the sun.

Everywhere were grapevines to keep off the summer heat. From the house, another young monk appeared. Over the top of a low-wall, I could see the roofs and domes of central Karyes some way below.

FR. C APPEARS

"Wait here," my guide said. He had a short conversation with a monk who appeared, and I thought that at last I had made contact. Then the young monk picked up his burden, a basket of fruit, and walked out of the gate and down the lane. My guide stopped for a moment, then shouted up to the house. Nothing happened. I waited. A minute or two later he shouted again. Still nothing happened. A third attempt was necessary some five minutes later.

A window opened upstairs and a dark face looked out. It was the *Protos,* a monk probably still in his thirties, and with very black hair. A short conversation followed, then the head disappeared inside again. Two or three minutes later, the *Protos* appeared from the imposing front door of the house. My guide gave him Neboysha's letter, which he read quickly.

"*I am sorry,*" he said, "*I cannot interpret for you. Too much to do. But do you need somewhere to sleep?*" "*No,*" I told him somewhat regretfully; I had by then found a bed in the hotel. "*I am very sorry, then,*" he said.

That was my first and only meeting with the *Protos.* I had no interpreter, but I had somewhere to sleep: the hotel of bitter waters. Certainly, it was a hotel that is totally unique. For about two-pounds a night, it provides monastic emptiness –without monastic consolations. Being weak, I have made great efforts since then to avoid staying there ever again. If there is a virtue in suffering, an understanding of fathers such as Theophan makes it clear that it is virtuous not in itself, but only when it leads to inner transformation: only when it leads us to God. This does underline a fact that may not have been clear before, that the monastic method does not give priority to the emptiness; the essential factor is that something else should fill it when we experience the consolation of divine-grace.

This is explained, in the way Maximos the Confessor put it, by a simple psychological formula which tells us*: "Such pain (which he a many fathers regarded as the 'reward' of meaningless plea sure) drives out unnatural pleasure, but does not totally destroy it. Its total destruction is effected by the grace of divine pleasure when this is active in the nous..."*

A few lines later, he says again that*: "... the cultivation of virtue produces dispassion (apatheia) in one's will, but not in one's nature. But when dispassion has been attained in one's will, the grace of divine pleasure becomes active in the nous."* (St. Maximos the Confessor in Volume 2 of *The Philokalia: The Complete Text)*

After the service and the shortness of my meeting with the *Protos,* I was somewhat despondent as I started my walk back down the track towards the town center and an evening of enforced silence.

As I approached the hotel, I met John, the Greek Australian I had been talking to earlier. We took another walk around the town, both I think glad of the chance to talk English. He told me how he had come with his Father to spend some time on the Island of Cythera, where they would rebuild the family home. His companion was the Abbot, now the only permanent occupant of the monastery near their home, a monastery that served today more as a parish church, rather than as a monastic community – although Father Meletius, its *geron,* was a sincerely religious man, as I later discovered in conversation. The Father was coming to the Holy Mountain to visit an old friend, George, Abbot of Gregoriou.

But now, Abbot Meletius was resting. John and I continued our walk. He explained to me that he had come with his friend and geron to the Holy Mountain as a representative of a group of young-Orthodox in Australia, in order to discover whether they could encourage some monastic activity there, where they found the life of the church somewhat lacking in intensity.

I have not heard the end of this story, but certain things I have heard lead me to believe that this pilgrimage was answered, and that Mount Athos now maintains some kind of presence at the antipodes. Finally, the conversation turned to my problem with translation. He could help, said my friend. If his geron would agree, he would be able to come with me to Father Paisios next morning, before I must catch the bus back to Dafni and the beginning of my journey back to England.

CHAPTER 18

ANOTHER VISIT TO ELDER PAISIOS

Elder Paisios (Convent - Souroti)

Thus it came about that, just after six the next morning, I walked down the outside-staircase of the hotel, through the never-closed rusty iron gate, and onto the street, where, in two minutes, my companion appeared. Knowing that the hermit's cell lay beyond the monastery of Koutloumousiou, we began walking across the square, past the shuttered shops and the Protaton, down a narrow lane to the point where it divided, one branch sign-posted for Dafni, the other for Koutloumousiou. The path lay through the outer part of Karyes, past ruined-buildings, and over a small bridge, opening to a long valley that sloped downhill.

We continued on up, out of the town, and climbing up the lower slope on the far side of the valley, until we came to an ornate stone-gateway across the muddy track. Here was the normal Athonite stone-seat, surrounded by sweet-chestnut peelings where somebody had stopped.

Rising over the fields, we could see in the distance the high stone walls of the monastery. In front of them lay walled and fenced vineyards, as well as occasional smaller buildings. I began to hear a mule bell in the distance. Shortly, a muleteer appeared round a bend in the track leading a string of four laden mules.

"Careful," he called out, "the last one kicks." My guide translated for me, and quickly we pressed ourselves against the wire fence at the side of the track. We continued on to the great stone drinking-fountain opposite the monastery gate, stopping to study the paths that opened up from that point. One track led to the right, two went straight ahead, then forked a short-way down, and it was there that we were as yet uncertain. As we approached, the problem solved itself, the divided paths met again a little further on. We continued, walking between drystone walls in terrain little different in character, flora, or the layout of its buildings, from the Forest of Dean where we had lived – except for the great number of sweet-chestnuts.

The track meandered-on for some way, passing log-gates to stone-built kellia. Tiny painted signs pointed to two small communities that lay along the track, and also to the hermit we had come to see. The path moved into the aisles of the chestnut forest. Finally, we came to a gate, and then a rough stile just before another rambling house. Now the signs pointed in two directions. Here we left the mule track and, climbing over the style, walked across the cropped grass into the trees, following a track worn by many pilgrims.

This took us down into a little valley overshadowed by some of the tallest, straightest chestnuts I have seen yet, and over a small stream. Climbing up the far bank, we glimpsed a group of tall, dark cypresses in the distance. Among them was a cottage on the top of a small hillock above the stream. As we approached, I saw that the cottage was surrounded by a high chain-link fence all the way round, at a distance of about eighty-feet.

Where the path met the fence was a gate, a handwritten notice, a string to a bell on the cottage veranda, a jar with a pencil and scraps of paper, and short tree stumps as seats for those who had to wait. All around was the silence of the forest. Translated, the pencilled note read: "Write what you would like, and put the note in the box, and I will help you more by prayer than with a lot of talk. I didn't come here to be a teacher."

We pulled the string, and heard a bell jangle. Then we waited: five-minutes; ten-minutes; nothing happened. We rang again, then waited again. Just as our attention lapsed, there was a muffled shout from the cottage. "Who is it? What do you want?"

My guide explained I was an Anglos come to see the Geron, an Englishman. There was brief pause, then a key sliding down a string. We unlocked the gate, entered, and locked it again. Up the path beside the cottage we went, and round the rear to the door. It was open, and, with smiling greeting, there was the *Geron*, Father Paisios, a small man, with hair just turning to gray, and a monk's cap that looked as if hand-knitted. Not very impressive at first glance, yet as I came to know him, I realized that more than what he says, it was what he is which is so helpful.

But I do not know how to explain this. Modern language is not enough. No words are enough, as he said to us. It was something he showed to us. Briefly, my guide explained who I was and why I had come. We were invited in, down a short passage past the door of a small chapel, and so into the main room of the *kelli*. This room was a perfect-square, about ten foot by ten, whitewashed inside, with a single door and a single window. Inside was an iron bedstead, an iron-stove, a mantlepiece with several icons, a rough plank-bench round two-sides, with one small armchair made of rough-sawn logs.

There was little else in the room except the rudiments of hospitality: three stainless steel mugs, a jug of water, and a box of loukoumi. The *geron* supplied us each with water and loukoumi, then left the room, returning after a few moments with a canvas bag from which he withdrew the familiar wool and small tools with which so many monks on the mountain earn their frugal-bread by making prayer-ropes – rosaries with woollen knots instead of beads.

The Father, the Mountain's then only generally recognized elder, began answering my questions by giving me 'something to be said to everyone,' as he put it, presumably to our English-speaking world,

"*You English and the other Western nations are too logical*" he told me.

"*You have done much good by spreading the results of your ability to think – by giving the world practical benefits of technology: machines, nuts and bolts, etc. But if you could now become a source of good heart to the world, it would be better.*"

"*Yet first you yourselves need to be of good heart. This restoration of the heart is above all what is needed in the West. This would be of incalculable benefit to the world.*"

To many people in the West, this idea, and the idea of the over-intellectualism and the dependence on words that go with it, are not new – but I had become increasingly aware that, while today teachings abound about how to alter our thought, it is these that we must transcend. What we need is ways of changing the heart.

The remainder of this conversation with him provided some of the practical clues I needed if I was even to achieve my own aim of emotional renewal, although it would be a long time before I even understood this.

TRYING TOO HARD

The approach was learned in part from other conversations, observations and experiences on the Holy Mountain in September and October of that year, and in part from Elder Paisios, and is possibly new to Western thought. Still talking to me as individual, and I think also to the West in general, the elder told me: "You try too hard!" This was nothing new. I was first told more than twenty years earlier that I try too hard. I have said the same to others, and learned to recognize all this as symptomatic of over-activity by the 'talking' part of the mind. It is true: on the rare occasions, when the 'talking mind' does really try, it tries too hard.

So to 'put our heart into things' once again, we must first find means of escaping from the guardian Cerberus of the talkative part, we need to break-free from the psychological habits that maintain its dominance. The greatest of these guardians, according to the Early Fathers, was pride. In pride, we believe we can make our own shape for our lives ... and this attitude of pride lends a spurious authority to our thinking.

To resolve this, we must begin from where we are: from our own thoughts. Only by breaking the authority of words, by getting the 'doing' mind to stop being active for a moment, can we wake the heart, for the characteristic of our 'dominant side,' formed while we are young, I think, is that its compulsive-overactivity overlays our natural capacity to speak and act 'from the heart.' 'Dominant-side prayer' too is pointless in itself, (although it can lead to true prayer), so instead of forcing ourselves to sterile prayer which, through disappointment, dries up the desire for prayer, we should learn eventually to pray only to the dictates of the heart. And we may perhaps be able to waken these in the way described in the next paragraphs. This may lead to prayer or study in a different way – arising from a different part of ourselves.

ACTIONS OF THE HEART

Now the *Geron* gave me instruction that many people – but perhaps not all – think they can follow. He told me to think of him as a doctor, who can prescribe for maladies of the spirit. But what he said is difficult to put into writing. Sometimes perhaps people need personal guidance as to the meaning of these difficult words.

These instructions helped to make clear to me certain aspects of the idea of *thlipsis* and other related questions that had been discussed earlier. These have to be understood in a particular way, and can easily be misunderstood. In fact, these ideas should finally be approached and put into practice only after direct face-to-face communication with someone who regularly practices them. Until one has done this, one should not try to interpret them in any final way.

Because of this, it has not been possible to put every detail into this book, but I hope to have included sufficient to allow these things to be recognized by those who have previous experience.

For many of us, the basis of these instructions lies within our reach if only we can remember certain moments we have already experienced: those moments when we are, by some failure of ours, or some good action by others, made clearly and emotionally aware of our own inadequacy, our own unwillingness, and so on. This can happen when we hear of, or more rarely, observe some noble act or example which appears to be beyond our own normal ability: charity; heroism; unselfishness; self-sacrifice. Sometimes this experience inspires, sometimes it falls on the wrong part of our mind, and then it simply feels uncomfortable.

And if we are unable to escape thought, we should think of the good works of others, the 'examples given us by God,' as Father Paisios described them, and then, in comparison to those, think about all the wrong we ourselves have done, and simply allow the resulting discontent with ourselves – the emotion known by the Desert Fathers as *katanyxis* (compunction) to emerge within us.

Then, perhaps, we may discover the meaning of the elder's words.

KATANYXIS

Stone steps, Gregoriou (MG)

"Blessed are they that mourn, for they shall be comforted."
*(*Matthew 5:4*)*

This difficult practice, seen as a means of 'waking the heart,' links with the idea of 'becoming oneself' and its converse, hamartia, which is to act while ignoring the heart. So it is also 'failure to become oneself,' since one becomes more oneself only by waking the heart. *Katanyxis*, evoked in the way described by Father Paisios, is one form of such an awakening. Many forms of the despair and 'Protestant guilt,' which are such a feature of our modern psyche, on the other hand, become ways of lulling the heart to sleep.

I discovered this only because, in some way, this idea of *katanyxis* complemented the experiences of the two earlier and incomplete visits to Athos on this trip, where I went through all kinds of different experiences involving thunderstorms, arousing fear, self-doubt, and other difficult feelings. Through these situations, I found myself learning more about the different kinds of *thlipsis*. I discovered that *katanyxis* – elsewhere I think called 'remorse of conscience' – is entirely different from fears created by circumstance, and especially from all fears and inhibitions caused by externally applied disciplines. Such externally-induced fears cloud the mind and emotions ... and the Early Fathers of the Church, seen without interpretation, correctly stated that nothing which excites or clouds the mind is of God.

True compunction can therefore be recognized by its opposite effect, that it awakens the heart without excitement, and because of its unifying quality, evokes a different and more flexible quality of conscience. This changes our 'wanting.'

It cuts to a quite different 'place' in us from that reached by threat of punishment: brings the right emotions to the point of prayer, so that we truly want to pray, and so creates a different self awareness, a different, more-direct and in some way more-motivating self-knowledge, and this motivating or emotional quality is of great importance both because it leads us in time to change behavior, and because it forms the entry point for a change in our hearts. This is sometimes experienced by every emotionally normal person.

The experience of *katanyxis* is virtually identical with those moments of discomfort, when hearing about some person or some action of exceptional 'goodness,' when we feel a sincere discontent with our own performance.

The point is that, instead of avoiding this *'aynbite of inwit'* – a medieval English term for conscience – we can encourage it. We can pray to God for it, and that prayer is one that may be answered.

This *katanyxis* has a very definite quality, a 'taste' which we can learn to recognize. It is a kind of constructive remorse: something which can give us the strength to pray and so can, in this and other ways, change the direction of our lives. It is more common in childhood memories than amongst the muddled recollections which come later, but if we learn to recognize it we can – with effort and by grace – hope to increase it.

Further light was shed onto this whole subject when I talked to one of the men who today follows the instruction laid down by Saint Silouan earlier in this century. The idea – referred to much earlier in the book – of keeping one's soul in hell – refers to the same thing. We all of us suffer from pride. This is especially a danger for those who have made some progress on the spiritual way, and particularly if they lack the protections of the monastic life. "*The idea of keeping your soul in hell,*" said the monk with whom I was discussing this, "is particularly related to pride. If you keep in mind your mistakes, your wrong actions, and allow this to make you unhappy, to arouse an emotional remorse at your failures (*harmatia*), then you have some means of eliminating this demon pride. But one must not take this so far that one despairs. One must take it in moderation, and when one gets too despondent, must cease this practice."

It is a matter of using it in measure, in order to hold a balanced or central-position. In this sense, the instructions of the geron Father Paisios were thus identical with those of St. Silouan half a century before. This same 'refuge from pride' had also been taught in different form by many earlier '*elders*:' St. Anthony, St. Sisoe, St. Makarios in his famous 'homilies,' and the Russian St. Pimen.

This is a difficult practice. It has not only to be understood but 'mastered,' and at first it is very easily misunderstood, a fact that explains the many times in the past when people have been overcome by the religious despair that arises when they overdo the practice of repentance. But few people today are in much danger from this, although inability to carry out this practice may form a basis for compunction.

SELF-CALMING

Normally, we soon learn to calm these qualms once again. This is why we fill our lives and our homes with distractions. These are only the outward signs of the jumbled inner furnishings, the false-personality all of us create within our minds. It is only in this kind of 'thinking about the examples,' and only if we avoid this trap of 'self-calming,' the escape in which we slip away into the false world of our imagination, that the heart is awoken. The compunction that then arises may perhaps provide the wellspring for a new direction.

Sometimes, this process of change of direction is gradual but progressive. But one problem is that suitable 'data' for creating this compunction are rarely available in our modern world. We need more 'good news' in the sense of news about good, unselfish actions. Many of us will also need other help before we can take this practice of compunction to the point of 'tears of remorse.'

As my experiences in the monasteries have shown me, this seed from the tree of life flowers in the Garden-of-Eden of the human heart – and does so best in an atmosphere of *koinonia*, sometimes translated community, sometimes communion, depending on context. This is the condition in which it responds most valiantly to the 'invisible' action of the Spirit.

EPILOGUE

Later, I wrote many things about that time. Even more recently I met an Englishman who shared my experience of the mountains, forests, and spiritual communities of Greece's Mount Athos. Each of us recognized the other's memories of that Holy Mountain as if they were our own, not only in similarity, but in identity. When one spoke to the other of it, the other recognized a memory we both remembered. Such memory reflects what can be called recognition knowledge.

– Robin Amis

View over the roofs of Monastery Gregoriou (MG)

APPENDIX

Letter of Laissez-Passer ('let pass') for Robin Amis

Issued by the Monastery of Gregoriou
Mount Athos, Greece
May 18, 1985

Original document

English translation:

On behalf of our entire brotherhood of the monastery, we are issuing a document recognizing Henry Robin Amis, an English Orthodox Christian, known by the name of Giorgios, passport number 754517, designating him as a Synergatis (fellow worker, and equal to the monks), and ask that he be given free access, both coming in and going out of the Holy Mountain.

This is issued from the entire community (brotherhood) of the Monastery of Gregoriou.

GLOSSARY OF GREEK TERMS

AGAPE *αγάπη* : love

AGION OROS *Αγιο(ν) Ορος* : the Holy Mountain

AGRYPNIA *Αγρυπνία* : Vigil service

ALITHEA *αλήθεια* : Truth (the opposite of lithe or forgetfulness)

ANTIDORON *αντίδωρο(ν)* : blessed bread given after
    communion

APATHEIA *απάθεια* : dispassion

ARCHONTARIS *αρχοντάρης* : guest-master

ARSANAS *αρσανάς* : port entrance to monastery

ASKESIS *άσκησις ;* asceticism with obedience and understanding

CAIQUE *καΐκι* : traditional Aegean fishing boat

CHRISTOS ANESTI! ALITHOS ANESTI! *Χριστός ἀνέστη!*
Ἀληθῶς ἀνέστη! : Christ is risen! He is risen indeed!
    (Paschal greeting)

DIAMONITIRION *Διαμονητήριο(ν)* : official pass
    for visitors to the Holy Mountain

DIKAIOS *Δίκαιος* : righteous man

ELEISON ME *Ελέησόν με!* : have mercy on me!

EPIKLESIS *επίκλησις* : consecretion of the Holy Bread

GERON *γέρων* : Elder

GERONTES *γέροντες* : plural of Geron, Elders

GERONTIKON *Γεροντικόν* : compilation of sayings of the Elders

GIGANTES *γίγαντες* : large beans

GNOSIS *γνώσις* : spiritual knowledge/ knowledge of God

HAMARTIA *ἁμαρτία* : an error of judgment, failure, sin,
    missing the mark, as in the Parable of the Talents

HEGUMEN *Ηγουμένη* : (fem.) HEGUMENOS *Ηγούμενος* :
    (mas.) the abbot of a monastery

HESYCHAST *ησυχαστής* : monk who practices hesychia

HESYCHIA *ησυχία* : a mystical tradition of experiential prayer
    in the Orthodox Church.

HYPOMONIE *υπομονή* : patience

ICONOSTASIS *εκονοστάστιο* : screen in Orthodox sanctuary
    separating the nave from the altar

KALISPERA *καλησπέρα!* : Good evening

KATANYXIS *κατάνυξις* : remorse of conscience

KATHOLIKON *καθολικό(ν)* : main church of a monastery

KELLI *κελλί* : *(sing.)* KELLIA *κελλιά* : (pl.)
    a small monastic community

KOINONIA *κοινωνία* : community/communion

KONACHI *κονάκι* : monastic dwelling in Karyes

KYRIE IESOU CHRISTE YIE TOU THEOU ELEISON ME TON
AMARTOLON *Κύριε Ἰησού Χριστέ / Υἱὲ του Θεού ελέησόν με
τον ἁμαρτωλόν* : Lord Jesus Christ, Son of God, have mercy on
me, a sinner.

LITHE *λήθη* : forgetfulness

LOGOI *λόγοι* : (plural for *λόγος*) the word of God

LOUKOUMI *λουκούμι* : Greek sweetmeat

LYPI *λύπη* : sorrow for one's sins

MACARONIA *μακαρόνια* : macaroni

MACROPROSOPOS *Μακροπρόσωπος* :
    Great (Divine) Countenance

MEGALOSCHEMA *μεγαλόσχημα* :
    advanced stage of monasticism

METAMELIA *μετάμελεια* : related to metanoia,
    transforming the stream of consciousness, repentance

METANOIA *μετάνοια* : repentance

METOCHI *μετόχι* : dependency of a monastery in the world

MICROPROSOPOS *μικροπρόσωπος* : Smaller Countenance

MNEME THANATOU *μνήμη θανάτου* : remembrance of death.

MNEME THEOU *μνήμη Θεού* : remembrance of God

MYSTERIA *μυστήρια* : the Sacraments

NEPSIS *νήψις* : wakefulness, watchfulness

NOUS *νούς* : the higher intelligence or reason,
    the mind's eye (nonverbal part of the mind)

ORTHROS *όρθρος* : Matins, morning service held prior to the
    Divine Liturgy

PEIRASMOS *πειρασμός* : temptation

PHILOKALIA *Φιλοκαλία* : love of beauty, name of a collection
    of spiritual instructions from the Eastern Christian tradition.

PHILOXENIA *φιλοξενία* : hospitality

POLYELEOS *πολυέλαιος* : large moving Church chandelier

PROLEPSIS (sing.) *πρόληψη* : PROLEPSEIS (pl.) *προλήψεις* : predispositions

PROSEFCHI *προσευχή* : prayer

PROSOCHI *προσοχή* : take care

PROSOPON *πρόσωπο* : countenance (person), person-hood

PROSPHORA *πρόσφορα* : dedicated bread baked especially for the Holy Eucharist, given to the laity after the Liturgy

PROTATON *Πρωτάτο(ν)* : Administrative center of Athos.

PROTOS *Πρώτος* : Primate of Athos

RAKI *ρακί* : liqueur made from grape residue

SEMANTRON *Το σήμαντρο(ν)* : wooden plank (when struck) to call to services

SKETI (sing.) *σκέτη* : SKETES (pl) *σκέτες* : small monastic communities for advanced monks

SYGATATHESIS *συγκατάθεση* : voluntary response to temptation

SYNERGIA *συνέργια* : mutual cooperation/working together

THEORIA *θεωρία* : knowledge of God (not theory about God)

THEOSIS *Θέωση* : Deification – union with God

THLIPSIS *θλίψη* : sorrow, affliction

TO PERIVOLI TIS PANAGIAS *Το περιβόλι της Παναγίας* : name for the Holy Mountain (Mary's Garden)

TRAPEZA *τράπεζα* : dining room

TRISAGION *Τρισάγιον* : three Times Holy, a triple invocation honoring the Holy Trinity, a brief memorial service

TYPIKON *τυπικόν* : rule of monastic services

XENOS *ξένος* : foreigner

CPSIA information can be obtained at www.ICGtesting.com
Printed in the USA
BVOW11s1735140714

359060BV00001B/1/P